Gradual Psalms

Alleluia Verses and Tracts

For

Year A

Church Hymnal Series VI, Part I

Compiled By

Richard Crocker

For

The Standing Commission on Church Music

THE CHURCH HYMNAL CORPORATION
800 Second Avenue
New York, New York   10017

Gradual Psalms
Alleluia Verses and Tracts

INTRODUCTION

An important aspect of liturgical renewal has been the increased use of psalmody in our worship. The three-year Eucharistic lectionary includes a wide selection of Psalms, providing possibilities for singing Psalms in various ways. This collection of Gradual Psalms, Alleluia Verses and Tracts consists of Psalm verses with Refrains, and provides an opportunity to participate in the ancient tradition of responsorial singing of the Psalms.

Psalmody at the gradual restores the tradition of having a cantor sing verses selected from a Psalm, while the congregation responds with a refrain; this tradition can be directly connected to Hebrew practice.

Proper Gregorian gradual melodies are usually extremely ornate, and unsuitable for typical modern parish use. In searching for a practical congregational psalmody, we turn to simpler, less elaborate Gregorian melodies. These have been preserved from ancient times, only in music for the offices (Matins, Lauds, Vespers, etc.) and not for the Holy Eucharist, and in the style of *antiphonal psalmody*, not *responsorial psalmody*. The solution to the problem of providing easily sung congregational gradual psalmody, as found in this collection, is to use the simpler forms and styles of office antiphonal psalmody, but having them sung by solo cantor and congregation in a responsorial style.

The compelling reason for doing this is the great value — practical, musical, and spiritual — of using these antiphon (refrain) melodies. They represent one of the most ancient traditions of Christian musical experience in a compact and accessible form. These priceless jewels of pure melody, many so short as to be sung in a single breath, seem to represent everything needed for our immediate purpose of congregational refrains for proper Psalms in the Eucharist.

The ancient repertory of Office antiphons (dating from the period circa A.D. 400-700), which is used as the source of the refrains in this collection, consists of melodies that are used again and again throughout

the Latin Office for many different texts. This fact
indicates that these antiphons are a broad, deep foun-
dation of Christian song. Because of this, it is rela-
tively easy to adapt these melodies for modern English
usage.

GUIDES FOR USE

A Psalm Tone has five parts, as shown in this
example:

TONE VI

Into- nation	1st Reci- ting Note	Mediant Cadence	2nd Reci- ting Note	Final Cadence (Ending)

The *Intonation* is sung to the first two syllables of each verse which follows the Refrain, and is
indicated in the text by italics. The Intonation is not
sung at the beginning of the second or third verse of a
group of verses.

The *1st Reciting Note* is used for all syllables
of the first half of the verse which are not sung to

the Intonation or to the Mediant Cadence, including
the initial syllables of the second or third verse of
a group of verses.

The _Mediant Cadence_ comes before the asterisk
in the Psalm text, and consists of one or two accents,
and one, two, or three preparatory syllables. Accent
marks in the Psalm text (ˊ) correspond to accent marks
under the notes in the Psalm Tone (♪). The notes in
parenthesis are used as needed between the syllables
with accent marks, or between the last accented syllable and the end of the half verse. Preparatory syllables follow the diagonal bar (/) in the text; they
are sung to the notes following the diagonal bar under
the music.

In a few cases, the first half of the verse
ends with an accented syllable. This should be sung to
the final accented note in the first half of the Psalm
Tone, omitting the note in parenthesis and the last
note of the Mediant Cadence. (When this happens, it is
considered an _abrupt mediation._)

In some Psalm Tones, two (and in some cases,
three or four) notes are slurred together. These should

never be divided between two syllables. Words or syllables requiring two or more notes are indicated by
dots over the syllables in the pointed text (e.g.,
set up-on your thröne [for Psalm Tone I *d*]).

The *2nd Reciting Note* is used like the first,
and the *Final Cadence* is used like the *Mediant Cadence*.

In a few cases, due to the shortness of the
half verse, the Intonation or the Reciting Note is
omitted. This is indicated in the pointed text by the
use of a dash (——) (e.g., O LÖRD —— God öf hosts).

In some cases it has not been possible to
align the real accents of the English text with the
accented notes of the Psalm Tone. In such cases, the
accent marks over the syllables in the pointed text
indicate how the syllable goes with the notes.

+ + + +

The Refrain and Psalm Tone are sung in the following
manner:

1. The Refrain is sung first by a cantor.
2. The Refrain is then immediately repeated by
   the congregation and choir.
3. Each Psalm verse, or group of verses, is sung
   by the cantor.
4. The Refrain is repeated by the congregation
   and choir after each verse or group of verses,
   as indicated in the pointed text.

The Alleluia with its Verses is sung in a similar
manner:

1. The Alleluia is sung first by a cantor.
2. The Alleluia is then repeated by the congregation and choir.
3. The Verse is sung by the cantor.
4. The Alleluia is repeated by the congregation
   and choir.

The Tract may be sung by the cantor throughout; or

begun by the cantor and continued by the congregation

and choir.

The Refrains should be sung in a natural,

flowing manner, without undue accents or change of pace.

They can be faster or slower, or otherwise varying in

character according to the text, the season, or the oc-

casion. Many Refrains can be sung as one phrase without

stopping for breath. Others have a natural division of

sense, marked by a half bar, where a breath may be taken.

Refrains should follow the Psalm verses without hesita-

tion.

Choosing a comfortable pitch for both cantor

and the people is very important. In this collection,

Refrains and Psalm Tones often have been transposed into

a comfortable range, but additional transpositions might

be necessary.

The Gradual Psalm could be thought of as a second Old Testament reading, which is normally sung rather than read, and the people's response to this reading is the Refrain. The cantor should sing the Psalm verses in full view of the congregation, from the lectern or pulpit, or from some other visible location where the other lessons are read. The congregation should remain seated for the Gradual Psalm, as they do for other readings. The Gloria Patri is not added to the Gradual Psalm verses, since this is a continuation of the reading from the Old Testament.

The Alleluia Verse (or Tract) may be sung by the cantor from the choir, and may follow or be followed by a hymn. The congregation stands for the singing of the Alleluia (and hymn) and remains standing for the Gospel.

The Refrains, Verses, Alleluias and Tracts are normally sung without accompaniment, but a convenient manner of performance in many parishes and missions would be to have the organ (or other instrument) play the complete Refrain or Alleluia melody before it is sung by the cantor. It is then sung by the cantor alone, then repeated by congregation and choir, and continued according to the directions above. It might be helpful for the organ (or other instrument) to play the Refrain in unison octaves while the congregation sings, until the melody is known well enough to be sung without instrumental assistance. In some situations, it might be possible to ring bells during Refrains and Alleluias, either in a set pattern, or at random. The verses should be sung without any accompaniment.

In some places, and during certain times of the year, it may be preferable to have the verses sung by two or three cantors, or even by the entire choir. When the people have become familiar with this style of singing the Psalm verses, it might be desirable to urge the entire congregation to join in singing the verses as well as the Refrains and Alleluias.

As in other parts of the Eucharist, the use of psalmody in the Service of the Word allows flexibility and a freedom of choice: the text for the Refrains is not a part of the Lectionary, and other Refrains and Psalm verses may be used in place of the ones used in this collection. While the shorter selection of verses, as found in the Lectionary, is usually sung at the Gradual in the Eucharist, in some situations a larger part of the Psalm, or the entire Psalm, may be sung. Some congregations may wish to sing a seasonal Refrain, using the same Refrain — words and music — throughout a season of the Church Year. In other places, it might be preferable to repeat the same Gradual Psalm through-out a particular season. Other musical forms and styles, of course, may be used in the singing of both Refrains and Verses. Some congregations may wish to use harmo-nized chant (Anglican Chant) for the Verses with the Refrains in unison; in other places, forms of modern chant may be used; in still other congregations, the Psalms may be sung in metrical versions.

This collection provides music which has been sung by the Church for many centuries, and it is hoped that this music will continue to be sung for years to come. Through the use of these ancient Refrains and Psalm Tones, it is hoped that the contemporary and future Church will look upon this traditional song of the Church not only as a fitting way to sing the Psalms, but also as a model and inspiration for the creation of new liturgical psalmody.

The complete Gradual Psalms will appear as Church Hymnal Series VI in the following parts:

Part I   - Year A

Part II - Year B

Part III - Year C

Part IV - Holy Days, The Common of Saints and for Various Occasions

Part V   - *Lesser Feasts and Fasts* and selected Psalms from *The Book of Occasional Services*

These Psalms will be issued in the following order:

Part I
Part IV
Part II
Part III
Part V

The Standing Commission on Church Music expresses deepest appreciation to the many congregations, clergy and musicians who have included representative items from this collection in their services, and have offered many helpful suggestions, many of which have been incorporated in this publication. We are especially grateful to Dr. Richard Crocker for his research and preparation of the psalmody and for his assistance in the preparation of the introduction to the collection. The refrain texts represent the research and work of Captain Howard Galley, C.A.. The Commission is most grateful to him, to the Reverend Ronald V. Haizlip and to members of the Standing Commission on Church Music Service Music Committee who prepared the manuscript which has been used for this publication of the psalmody.

1 Advent A

Refrain

I was glad when they said to me,

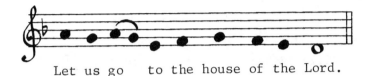

Let us go   to the house of the Lord.

Psalm 122   Tone I*f*

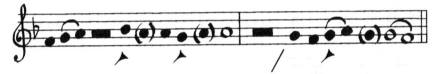

2 *Now our* —— féet are stánd-ing*
 within your gates, / O Je-rü-sa-lëm.
3 Jerusalem is búilt as a ći-ty*
 that is at u- / ni-ty with it-sëlf;
4 To which the tribes go up,
 the tríbes of thé LORD,*
  the assembly of Israel,
  to praise the / Name of thé LORD.

REFRAIN

5 *For thére* are the thrónes of júdg-ment,*
 the thrones of the / house of Dä-vïd.
6 Pray for the peáce of Je-rú-sa-lem:*
 "May they pros- / per who lóve yöu.
7 —— Peáce be with-ín your walls*
 and quiet- / ness with-ín your towers.

REFRAIN

8 *For mÿ* brethren añd com-pán-ions' sake,*
 I pray for / your pros-pér-i-tÿ.
9 Because of the house of the LÓRD our God,*
 I will / seek to dö you goöd."

REFRAIN

BCP, p. 779

1 ADVENT A

ALLELUIA VIII

Al-le - lu - ia, al-le-lu - ia, al - le-lu-ia.

VERSE (Psalm 85:7)   TONE VIIIg

Show us your mercy, O Lord,*   and grant us your

sal - va - tion.

2 ADVENT A

REFRAIN

In his time, jus-tice and peace shall flour-ish.

PSALM 72   TONE Ig

1 *Give the* King your jús-tice, Ó God,*
      and your righteousness / to the Kíng's Son;
2 That he may rule your péo-ple ríght-eous-ly*
      and the / poor with jús-tice;
                                    REFRAIN

3 *That the* mountains may bring prosperity tó the péo-ple,*
      and the little / hills bring right-eous-ness.
4 He shall defend the needy a-móng the péo-ple,*
      he shall rescue the poor and crush / the op-prés-sor.
                                    REFRAIN

5 *He shäll* live as long as the sún and móon en-dure,*
      from one generation / to an-óth-er.
6 He shall come down like rain up-ón the mówn field,*
      like showers that / wa-ter thë earth.
                                    REFRAIN

7 *In his* time shall the ríght-eous flóur-ish;*
      there shall be abundance of peace till the / moon
                  shall bë no more.
8 He shall rúle from séa to sea,*
      and from the River to the / ends of the earth.
                                    REFRAIN

BCP, p. 685

ALLELUIA I

Al-le-lu - ia, al-le-lu - ia, al-le - lu-ia.

VERSE (Luke 3:4,6)   TONE I*f*

Pre - pare the way of the Lord, make his paths straight;*

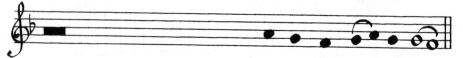

and all flesh shall see the sal-va-tion of our God.

3 ADVENT A

REFRAIN

Come, O Lord, and save us.

PSALM 146　　　　　　　　　　TONE Ig

4 *Hap-pÿ* are they who have the God of Já-cob fór
　　　their help!*
　　whose hope is / in the LÖRD their God;
5 Who made heaven and earth, the seas, and áll that
　　　is iń them;*
　　who keeps his prom- / ise for év-er;
　　　　　　　　　　　　　　　　REFRAIN

6 *Who gives* justice to thóse who are op-pressed,*
　　and food to / those who hún-ger.
7 The LORD sets the prisoners free;
　　the LORD opens the eýes of thé blind;*
　　the LORD lifts up those / who are bówed down.
　　　　　　　　　　　　　　　　REFRAIN

8 *The LÖRD* loves the righteous;
　　the LORD caŕes for the stŕan-ger;*
　　　he sustains the orphan and widow,
　　　but frustrates the way / of the wíck-ed.
9 The LORD shall réign for év-er,*
　　your God, O Zion, throughout all generations.
　　　/ Hal-le-lú-jah!
　　　　　　　　　　　　　　　　REFRAIN

BCP, p. 803.

3 Advent A

Alleluia IV

Al-le-lu-ia, al-le - lu - ia, al-le - lu-ia.

Verse (Luke 4:18)   Tone IV*e*

The Spir - it of the Lord is up-on me;*   he has

anointed me to preach good tid-ings to the   poor.

4 ADVENT A

REFRAIN

Lift up your heads, O gates; and the King of

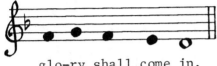

glo-ry shall come in.

PSALM 24   TONE I♩

1 *The eärth* is the LORD's and all that is in it,*
    the world and / all who dwell there-in.
2 For it is he who founded it up-on the seas*
    and made it firm upon the / riv-ers of the deep.

            REFRAIN

3 *"Who cän* ascend the hill of the LORD?*
    and who can stand / in his hö-ly pläce?"
4 "Those who have clean hands and a pure heart,*
    who have not pledged themselves to falsehood,
    nor sworn / by what is a fraud.

            REFRAIN

5 *They shäll* receive a bléss-ing from the LORD*
    and a just reward from the God of / their sal-vä-tiön."
6 Such is the generation of thóse who seék him,*
    of those who seek your face, O / God of Jä-cöb.

            REFRAIN

            BCP, p. 613

ALLELUIA III

Al-le - lu - ia, al-le - lu-ia, al-le - lu-ia.

VERSE (Matt. 1:23)   TONE III♭

A vir - gin shall con-ceive and bear a   son,*

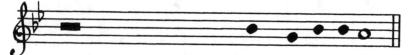

and his name shall be called Em-man-u-el.

CHRISTMAS DAY ABC I *(at midnight)*

REFRAIN

To-day is born our Sav-ior, Christ the Lord.

PSALM 96   TONE Va

1 *Sing to* the LORD a new song;*
   sing to the LORD, all the whole earth.
2 Sing to the LORD and bless his Name;*
   proclaim the good news of his sal-va-tion
      from day to day.

                        REFRAIN

3 *De - clare* his glory among the na-tions*
   and his wonders a-mong all peo-ples.
4 For great is the LORD and greatly to be praised;*
   he is more to be feared than all gods.

                        REFRAIN

11 *Let the* heavens rejoice, and let the earth be glad;
   let the sea thunder and all that is in it;*
     let the field be joyful and all that is there-in.

                        REFRAIN

12 *Then shall* all the trees of the wood shout for joy
   before the LORD when he comes,*
    when he comes to judge the earth.

                        REFRAIN

BCP, p. 725

CHRISTMAS DAY ABC I *(at midnight)*

ALLELUIA VIII

Al-le - lu - ia, al-le-lu - ia, al - le-lu-ia.

VERSE (Luke 2:10-11) TONE VIII*g*

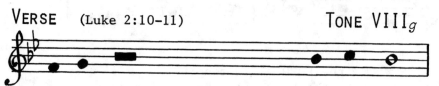

Be-hold, I bring you good tidings of great joy;*

to you is·born a Sav-ior, Christ the Lord.

CHRISTMAS DAY ABC II *(at dawn)*

REFRAIN

To us a child is born; to us a Son is giv-en.

PSALM 97   TONE VIIb

1 *The LORD* is King;
   let the earth re-joice;*
      let the multitude of the isles be glad.
2 Clouds and darkness are round a-bout him,*
      righteousness and justice are the foun-da-tions
                        of his throne.

REFRAIN

3 *A fire* —— goes be-fore him*
      and burns up his ene-mies on ev-ery side.
4 His light-nings light up the world;*
      the earth sees it and is a-fraid.

REFRAIN

11 *Light has* sprung up for the right-eous,*
      and joyful gladness for those who are true-heart-ed.
12 Rejoice in the LORD, you right-eous,*
      and give thanks to his ho-ly Name.

REFRAIN

BCP, p. 726

CHRISTMAS DAY ABC II *(at dawn)*

ALLELUIA II

Al -le-lu-ia, al-le-lu-ia, al-le-lu-ia.

VERSE (Luke 2:14)   TONE II

Glo-ry to God in the high-est,✻ and peace to his

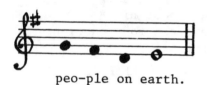

peo-ple on earth.

CHRISTMAS DAY ABC III *(during the day)*

REFRAIN

All the ends of the earth   have seen the

sal-va-tion of our   God.

PSALM 98   TONE VIIa

1 *Sïng tö* the LORD a new song,*
     for he has done mar-ve-lous thïngs.
2 With his right hand and his ho-ly arm*
     has he won for him-self the vïc-to-rÿ.

                                    REFRAIN

3 *The LORD* has made known his vic-to-ry;*
     his righteousness has he openly shown in
          the sight of the na-tions.
4 He remembers his mercy and faithfulness to
          the house of Is-ra-el,*
     and all the ends of the earth have seen the
          vic-to-ry of our Göd.

                                    REFRAIN

5 *Shöut wïth* joy to the LORD, all yöu lands;*
     lift up your voice, re-joice, and sïng.
6 Sing to the LORD with the harp,*
     with the harp and the voice of söng.

                                    REFRAIN

BCP, p. 727

CHRISTMAS DAY ABC III *(during the day)*

ALLELUIA II

Al - le-lu-ia, al-le-lu-ia, al-le-lu-ia.

VERSE (John 1:14)   TONE II

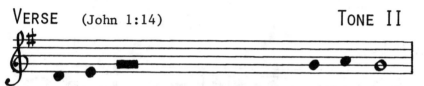

The Word was made flesh and dwelt a-mong us,*

full of grace and truth.

1 CHRISTMAS ABC

REFRAIN

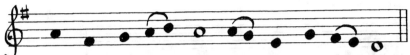

The Word was made flesh and dwelt a - mong us.

PSALM 147   TONE VII♭

13 *Wör - shïp* the LÓRD, O Je-rú-sa-lem;*
    praise your Gód, O Zí-on;
14 For he has strengthened the bárs of yóur gates;*
    he has blessed your chíl-dren with-ín you.

                                    REFRAIN

15 *He häs* established peáce on your bór-ders;*
    he satisfies yóu with the fín-est wheat.
16 He sends out his com-mánd to thé earth,*
    and his word runs vé-ry swíft-ly.

                                    REFRAIN

20 *He dë* - clares his wórd to Já-cob,*
    his statutes and his júdg-ments to Iś-ra-el.
21 He has not done so to any óth-er ná-tion;*
    to them he has not revealed his judgments.
    Hál-le-lú-jah!

                                    REFRAIN

BCP, p. 805

1 CHRISTMAS ABC

ALLELUIA II

Al - le-lu-ia, al-le-lu-ia, al-le-lu-ia.

VERSE (John 1:14)   TONE II

We have seen his glo-ry;* glory that is his as

the Fa-ther's on-ly Son.

Holy Name ABC

Refrain

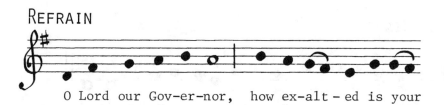

O Lord our Gov-er-nor, how ex-alt-ed is your

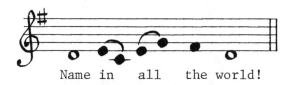

Name in all the world!

Psalm 8   Tone VIIb

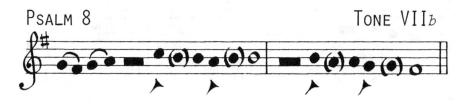

4 *When I* consider your heavens, the work of your fin-gers,*
    the moon and the stars you have set in their cour-ses,
5 What is man that you should be mind-ful of him?*
    the son of man that you should seek him out?

REFRAIN

6 *You have* made him but little lower than the an-gels;*
    you adorn him with glo-ry and hon-or;
7 You give him mastery over the works of your hands;*
    you put all things un-der his feet:

REFRAIN

8 —— All sheep and ox-en,*
    even the wild beasts of the field,
9 The birds of the air, the fish of the sea,*
    and whatsoever walks in the paths of the sea.

REFRAIN

BCP, p. 592

Holy Name ABC

Alleluia I

Al-le-lu - ia, al -le-lu - ia, al-le - lu-ia.

Verse   (Hebrews 1:1-2)   Tone I*f*

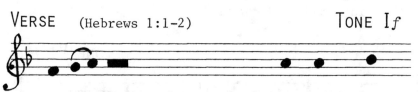

In the past God spoke to our fa-thers through

the pro-phets,* but now he has spo-ken to us

through his Son.

2 CHRISTMAS ABC

REFRAIN

How dear to me is your dwell-ing, O Lord of hosts!

PSALM 84   TONE VIIb

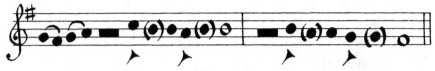

1 *My soül* has a desire and longing for the coúrts of
                          thé LORD;*
      my heart and my flesh re-jóice in the lív-ing God.
2 The sparrow has found her a house
      and the swallow a nest where shé may láy her young;*
      by the side of your altars, O LORD of hosts,
      my Kíng and mý God.

                                          REFRAIN

3 *Häp - p̈y* are they who dwéll in yóur house!*
      they will ál-ways be práis-ing you.
4 Happy are the people whose stréngth is iń you!*
      whose hearts are sét on the píl-grims' way.

                                          REFRAIN

5 *Thöse who* go through the desolate valley will fińd
                          it a pláce of springs,*
      for the early rains háve covered it with
                          poóls of wá-ter.
6 They will climb from héight to height,*
      and the God of gods will reveal him-sélf in Zí-on.

                                          REFRAIN

7 *LORD Göd* of hósts, hear mý prayer;*
      hearken, O Gód of Já-cob.
8 Behold our de-fénd-er, Ó God;*
      and look upon the face of yóur A-nóint-ed.

                                          REFRAIN

BCP, p. 707

ALLELUIA II

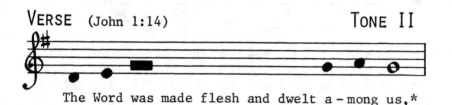

Al - le-lu-ia, al-le-lu-ia, al-le-lu-ia.

VERSE (John 1:14)   TONE II

The Word was made flesh and dwelt a-mong us,*

full of grace and truth.

EPIPHANY ABC

REFRAIN

All kings shall bow down be-fore him;

all the na-tions shall do him ser-vice.

PSALM 72   TONE VIIb

1 *Give the* King your jús-tice, Ó God,*
     and your righteousness tó the Kíng's Son;
2 That he may rule your péo-ple ríght-eous-ly*
     and the poór with jús-tice;

REFRAIN

8 *He shall* —— rúle from séa to sea,*
     and from the River to the eńds of thé earth.
10 The kings of Tarshish and of the íśles shall
               pay tríb-ute,*
     and the kings of Arabia and Sá-ba óf-fer gifts.

REFRAIN

12 *For he* shall deliver the poor who críes out iń dis-tress,*
     and the oppressed who hás no hélp-er.
13 He shall have pity on the lów-ly ańd poor;*
     he shall preserve the líves of the néed-y.

REFRAIN

17 *May his* Name remain for ever
     and be established as lóng as the sún en-dures;*
        may all the nations bless themselves in him and
             cáll him bléss-ed.

REFRAIN

BCP, p. 685

Epiphany ABC

Alleluia II

Al - le-lu-ia, al-le-lu-ia, al-le-lu-ia.

Verse (Matt. 2:2)   Tone II

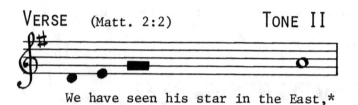

We have seen his star in the East,*

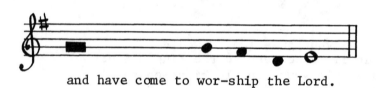

and have come to wor-ship the Lord.

1 Epiphany ABC

Refrain

I have found Da-vid my ser - vant; with my

ho - ly oil have I a-noint-ed him.

Psalm 89   Tone I𝑓

21 *My hand* will hóld hím fast*
    and my / arm will mäke him ströng.
22 No enemy shall de-céive him,*
    nor any wicked / man bring hím down.

REFRAIN

24 *My faith* - fulness and lóve shall bé with him,*
    and he shall be victori - / ous through mÿ Näme.
25 I shall make his do-mín-ion éx-tend*
    from the Great Sea / to the Rív-ër.

REFRAIN

26 *He will* say to me, 'Yóu are my Fá-ther,*
    my God, and the rock of / my sal-vä-tiön.'
27 I will make hím my fírst-born*
    and higher than the / kings of the eärth.

REFRAIN

28 *I will* keep my love for hím for év-er,*
    and my covenant / will stand firm for him.
29 I will establish his líne for év-er*
    and his throne as the / days of héav-ën.

REFRAIN

BCP, p. 715

1 Epiphany ABC

Alleluia III

Al-le - lu - ia, al-le -lu-ia, al-le - lu-ia.

Verse (Gal. 3:27)   Tone IIIa

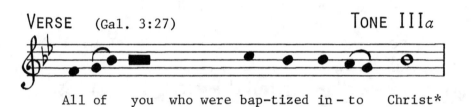

All of you who were bap-tized in - to Christ*

have clothed your-selves with Christ.

2 Epiphany A

Refrain

Be – hold, I come to do your will, O God.

Psalm 40   Tone II

1 *I wait* - ed patiently upon the LORD;*
   he stooped to me / and heárd my cry.
3 He put a new song in my mouth,
   a song of praise to our Gód;*
      many shall see, and stand in awe,
      and put their trust / in thé LORD.

REFRAIN

7 *In sac* - rifice and offering you take no pléas-ure*
   (you have given me ears / to heár you);
8 Burnt-offering and sin-offering you have nót re-quired,*
   and so I said, / "Be-hóld, I come.

REFRAIN

9 *In the* roll of the book it is written con-cérn-ing me;*
   'I love to do your will, O my God;
      your law is deep / in mý heart.'"
10 I proclaimed righteousness in the great
                        con-gre-gá-tion;*
      behold, I did not restrain my lips;
      and that, / O LORD, you know.

REFRAIN

BCP, p. 640

2 Epiphany A

Alleluia IV

Al-le-lu-ia, al-le - lu - ia, al-le - lu-ia.

Verse (John 1:29)   Tone IV*e*

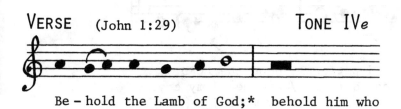

Be – hold the Lamb of God;* behold him who

takes a – way the sin of the world.

3 Epiphany A

REFRAIN

Lord, you have searched me out and known me.

PSALM 139   TONE IIIb

1 *You knŏw* my sitting down and my rís-ing up;*
   you discern my thoughts / from á-far.
2 You trace my journeys and my rést-ing-plăc̈-es*
   and are acquainted / with áll my ways.

                              REFRAIN

6 *Where căn* I go then frŏm your S̈pir-it?*
   where can I flee from / your prés-ence?
7 If I climb up to héav-en, yóu ar̈e there;*
   if I make the grave my bed, you are / there ál-so.

                              REFRAIN

8 *If Ï* take the wings of the mŏrn-ing*
   and dwell in the uttermost parts / of thé sea,
9 Even there your hánd will léad me*
   and your right / hand hóld me fast.

                              REFRAIN

10 *If Ï* say, "Surely the dárk-ness will cóv-er̈ me,*
    and the light around / me túrn to night,"
11 Darkness is not dark to you;
    the night is as bright as thë̈ day;*
    darkness and light to you / are bóth a-like.

                              REFRAIN

BCP, p. 794

3 Epiphany A

Alleluia VIII

Al-le - lu - ia, al-le-lu - ia, al - le-lu-ia.

Verse (Matt. 4:23)   Tone VIII*g*

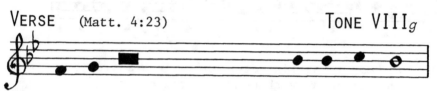

Je - sus preached the Good News of the king-dom;*

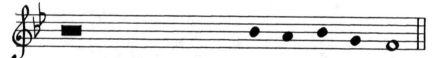

and healed every disease a - mong the peo - ple.

4 EPIPHANY A

REFRAIN

Put your trust in the Lord and do good.

PSALM 37   TONE IVe

1 *Do not* fret yourself because of / e-vil-do-ers;*
   do not be jeal- / lous of those who do wrong.
2 For they shall soon wither / like the grass,*
   and like the / green grass fade a-way.

REFRAIN

3 *Put your* trust in the LORD / and do good;*
   dwell in the land and / feed on its rich-es.
4 Take delight / in the LORD,*
   and he shall give / you your heart's de - sire.

REFRAIN

5 *Com - mit* your way to the LORD and / put
                              your trust in him,*
   and / he will bring it to pass.
6 He will make your righteousness as clear / as
                              the light*
   and your just deal- / ing as the noon-day.

REFRAIN

ALLELUIA - ad libitum   *BCP, p. 633*

REFRAIN

The Lord is my light and my sal-va-tion.

PSALM 27   TONE V*a*

1 *The LORD* is the strength of my life;*
   of whom then sháll I bé a-fraid?
2 When evildoers came upon me to eat up my flésh,*
   it was they, my foes and my adversaries, who
                  stúm-bled añd fell.

                                      REFRAIN

3 *Though an* army should encamp a-gáinst me,*
   yet 'my heart sháll not bé a-fraid;
4 And though war should rise up a-gáinst me,*
   yet will I pút my trúst in him.

                                        REFRAIN

5 *One thing* have I asked of the LORD;
   one thiñg I seek;*
      that I may dwell in the house of the LORD all
                    the dáys of mý life;
6 To behold the fair beauty of the LÓRD*
   and to seek him iñ his tém-ple.

                                        REFRAIN

7 *For in* the day of trouble he shall keep me safe
                  in his shél-ter;*
   he shall hide me in the secrecy of his dwelling
   and set me hígh up-oñ a rock.
9 Therefore will I offer in his dwelling an oblation
   with sounds of great glád-ness;*
   I will sing and make mú-sic tó the LORD.

                                        REFRAIN

          ALLELUIA - ad libitum   *BCP, p. 617*

REFRAIN

Hap - py are they who walk in the law of the Lord.

PSALM 119   TONE VI

9 *How shall* a young / man cleánse his way?*
   By keep- / ing tö yóur words.
10 With my whole heart / I séek you;*
   let me not stray from / your cöm-mánd-ments.

REFRAIN

11 *I treás* - ure your prom- / ise iń my heart,*
   that I may not / sin ä-gáinst you.
12 Bless-ed / are yóu, O LORD;*
   instruct me / in yöur stát-utes.

REFRAIN

13 *With my* lips / will I re-cite*
   all the judg- / ments öf yóur mouth.
14 I have taken greater delight in the way / of yóur
                    de-crees*
   than in all man- / ner öf ŕich-es.

REFRAIN

15 *I will* meditate on your / com-mánd-ments*
   and give atten- / tion tö yóur ways.
16 My delight is in / your stát-utes;*
   I will not / for-gët yóur word.

REFRAIN

ALLELUIA - ad libitum   *BCP, p. 764*

Refrain

I will re-call your right-eous-ness, O Lord.

Psalm 71   Tone VIIb

17 *Ö Göd,* you have taught me since I was young,*
    and to this day I tell of your won-der-fúl works.
18 And now that I am old and gray-headed, O God, do nót
        for-sáke me,*
    till I make known your strength to this generation
    and your power to áll who are to come.

REFRAIN

19 *Your right* - eousness, O God, reaches tó the heav-ens;*
    you have done great things;
    who is liké you, Ó God?
21 You strength-en me móre and more;*
    you en-fóld and cóm-fort me.

REFRAIN

22 *Thëre-före* I will praise you upon the lyre for your
        faith-ful-ness, Ó my God;*
    I will sing to you with the harp, O Holy One
        of Is-ra-el.
23 My lips will sing with jóy when I pláy to you,*
    and so will my soul, which yóu have re-deemed.

REFRAIN

ALLELUIA - ad libitum   *BCP, p. 684*

Refrain

For God a-lone my soul in si-lence waits.

Psalm 62   Tone VIII*g*

6 *For God* alone my soul in si-lence waits;*
   truly, my / hope is in him.
7 He alone is my rock and my sal-va-tion,*
   my stronghold, so that I shall / not be sha-ken.

                       REFRAIN

8 *In God* is my safety and my hon-or;*
   God is my strong rock / and my ref-uge.
9 Put your trust in him always, O peo-ple,*
   pour out your hearts before him, for God / is
               our ref-uge.

                       REFRAIN

13 *God has* spoken once, twice have I heard it,*
   that pow- / er be-longs to God.
14 Steadfast love is yours, O Lord,*
   for you repay everyone ac- / cord-ing to his deeds.

                       REFRAIN

ALLELUIA - ad libitum   *BCP, p. 669*

Last Epiphany A (The Transfiguration)

Refrain

Pro-claim the great-ness 'of the Lord our God;

he is the Ho-ly One.

Psalm 99   Tone VIIIg

1 *The LORD* is King;
   let the people trém-ble;*
      he is enthroned upon the cherubim;
      / let the eárth shake.
2 The LORD is great in Zí-on;*
      he is high a- / bove all péo-ples.

                                  REFRAIN

6 *Mo - ses* and Aaron among his priests,
   and Samuel among those who call up-ón his Name,*
      they called upon the LORD, / and he án-swered them.
7 He spoke to them out of the pillar of cloúd;*
      they kept his testimonies and the decree / that
                  he gáve them.

                                  REFRAIN

8 *"O LORD* our God, you answered thém in-deed;*
      you were a God who forgave them,
      yet punished them / for their é-vil deeds."
9 Proclaim the greatness of the LORD our God
   and worship him upon his hó-ly hill;*
      for the LORD our God / is the Hó-ly One.

                                  REFRAIN

                                  BCP, p. 728

Last Epiphany A (The Transfiguration)

Alleluia VIII

Al-le -lu -ia, al-le-lu -ia, al -le-lu-ia.

Verse (Matt. 17:5) Tone VIII*g*

This is my Son, my Be-lov-ed,* with whom I am

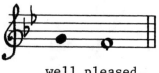

well pleased.

Ash Wednesday ABC

Refrain

The Lord re-mem-bers that we are but dust.

Psalm 103   Tone II

8 *The LORD* is full of compassion and mér-cy,*
    slow to anger and of / great kínd-ness.
9 He will not always ac-cúse us,*
    nor will he keep his anger / for év-er.

REFRAIN

10 *He has* not dealt with us according to our síns,*
     nor rewarded us according to / our wíck-ed-ness.
11 For as the heavens are high above the eárth,*
     so is his mercy great upon those / who féar him.

REFRAIN

12 *As far* as the east is from the wést,*
     so far has he removed / our síns from us.
13 As a father cares for his chíl-dren,*
     so does the LORD care for those / who féar him.

REFRAIN

BCP, p. 733

ASH WEDNESDAY ABC

TONE II

VERSE (2 Cor. 6:2)

> *Be-hold,* now is the acceptable time;*
> behold, now is the day of / sal-va-tion.

OR

TRACT (Psalm 130)

1 *Out of* the depths have I called to you, O LORD;
LORD, hear my voice;*
> let your ears consider well the voice
> > of my sup- / pli-ca-tion.

2 If you, LORD, were to note what is done a-miss,*
> O Lord, /.who could stand?

3 For there is forgiveness with you;*
> therefore / you shall be feared.

4 I wait for the LORD; my soul waits for him;*
> in his word / is my hope.

5 My soul waits for the LORD,
more than watchmen for the morn-ing,*
> more than watchmen for / the morn-ing.

6 O Israel, wait for the LORD,*
> for with the LORD there / is mer-cy;

7 With him there is plenteous re-demp-tion,*
> and he shall redeem Israel / from all their sins.

BCP, p. 784

1 Lent A

REFRAIN

Have mer-cy on me, O God, ac-cord-ing to

your lov-ing-kind-ness.

PSALM 51   TONE IVe

2 *Wash mḛ* through and through / from my ẅick-ed-ness*
   and / cleanse me frŏm m̈y sin.
3 For I know / my trans-grés-sions,*
   and my sin is / ev-er bë-fóre me.
                                                        REFRAIN

4 *A-gaínst* you only / have I sińned*
   and done what is / e-vil iñ yöur sight.
5 And so you are justified / when you spéak*
   and up- / right in yöur j̈údg-ment.
                                                        REFRAIN

6 *In-deḛd,* I have been wicked / from my bírth,*
   a sin- / ner from m̈y móth-ër's womb.
7 For behold, you look for truth / deep with-iń me,*
   and will make me under- / stand wis-döm śe-cr̈et-ly.
                                                        REFRAIN

8 *Purge mḛ* from my sin, and I / shall be púre;*
   wash me, and I / shall be clëan íñ-deed.
9 Make me hear of / joy and gláj-ness,*
   that the body you have / bro-ken m̈ay r̈e-joice.
                                                        REFRAIN

(continued)   BCP, p. 656

REFRAIN

Have mer-cy on me, O God, ac-cord-ing to

your lov-ing-kind-ness.

PSALM 51   TONE IVₑ

10 *Hide your* face / from my sins*
        and blot out / all my in-iq-ui-ties.
11 Create in me / a clean heart, O God,*
        and renew a right / spir-it with-in me.

                                    REFRAIN

12 *Cast me* not away / from your prés-ence*
        and take not your ho- / ly Spir-it from me.
13 Give me the joy of your / sav-ing help a-gain*
        and sustain me with your / boun-ti-fül Spir-it.

                                    REFRAIN

BCP, p. 656

1 LENT A

VERSE (Matt. 4:4)

Man shall not live by bréad a-lone,*
but by every word that proceeds
from / the moúth of God.

OR

TRACT   (Psalm 91)

1 *He who* dwells in the shelter of the Móst High,*
abides under the shadow of the / Al-míght-y.

2 He shall say to the LORD,
"You are my refuge and my stróng-hold,*
my God in whom / I pút my trust."

3 He shall deliver you from the snare of the húnt-er*
and from the dead - / ly pés-ti-lence.

4 He shall cover you with his pinions,
and you shall find refuge under his wíngs;*
his faithfulness shall be a shield / and búck-ler.

11 For he shall give his angels charge ó-ver you,*
to keep you / in áll your ways.

12 They shall bear you in their hánds,*
lest you dash your foot / a-gáinst a stone.

BCP, p. 719

2 LENT A

REFRAIN

Lord, let your lov-ing-kind-ness be up-on us,

as we have put our trust in you.

PSALM 33   TONE IV*e*

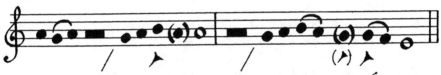

12 *Hap - py* is the nation whose God / is the LORD!*
      happy the people he has cho - / sen to be his own!
13 The LORD looks / down from heav-en,*
      and beholds all the / peo-ple in the world.

                                                      REFRAIN

14 *From where* he sits en - / throned he turns his gaze*
      on / all who dwell on the earth.
15 He fashions / all the hearts of them*
      and / un-der-stands all their works.

                                                      REFRAIN

18 *Be - hold,* the eye of the LORD is upon / those
                        who fear him,*
      on those who / wait up-on his love,
19 To / pluck their lives from death,*
      and to feed them / in time of fam-ine.

                                                      REFRAIN

20 *Our soul* waits / for the LORD;*
      he / is our help and our shield.
21 Indeed, our heart rejoic - / es in him,*
      for in his holy / Name we put our trust.

                                                      REFRAIN

                                          BCP, p. 626

TONE VIII*g*

VERSE (John 3:16)

> *God so* loved the world that he gave his ón-ly Son,*
>   that all who believe in him might have / e-tér-nal life.

OR

TRACT (Psalm 106)

1 *Give thanks* to the LORD, for hé is good,*
     for his mercy en - / dures for év-er.

2 Who can declare the mighty acts of the LORD*
     or / show forth áll his praise?

3 Happy are those who act with jús-tice*
     and always / do what iś right!

4 Remember me, O LORD, with the favor you have
                         for your péo-ple,*
     and visit me / with your sáv-ing help;

5 That I may see the prosperity of your elect
     and be glad with the gladness of your péo-ple,*
     that I may glory with / your in-hér-i-tance.

BCP, p. 741

3 LENT A

REFRAIN

To-day if you would hear his voice,

hard-en not your hearts.

PSALM 95   TONE II

6 *Come, let* us bow down, and bénd the knee,*
    and kneel before the LORD / our Mák-er.
7 For he is our God,
    and we are the people of his pasture and the
                            sheep of his hánd.*
    Oh, that today you would heark - / en tó his voice!

REFRAIN

8 *Hard - en* not your hearts,
    as your forebears did in the wíl-der-ness,*
    at Meribah, and on that day at Massah,
    when / they témpt-ed me.
9 They put me to the tést,*
    though they / had séen my works.

REFRAIN

10 *For - ty* years long I detested that generation and sáid,*
    "This people are wayward in their hearts;
    they do / not knów my ways."
11 So I swore in my wráth,*
    "They shall not enter in - / to mý rest."

REFRAIN

3 LENT A

TONE II

VERSE (John 4:42,15)

LORD, you are truly the Savior of the world;*
give me living water that I may nev - / er thirst
a-gain.

OR

TRACT (Psalm 42)

1 *As the* deer longs for the wa-ter-brooks,*
so longs my soul / for you, O God.

2 My soul is athirst for God, athirst for the liv-ing God;*
when shall I come to appear before
the pres - / ence of God?

3 My tears have been my food day and night,*
while all day long they say to me,
"Where / now is your God?"

4 I pour out my soul when I think on these things:*
how I went with the multitude and led them into / the
house of God,

5 With the voice of praise and thanks-giv-ing,*
among those who / keep ho-ly-day.

6 Why are you so full of heaviness, O my soul?*
and why are you so disquieqed / with-in me?

7 Put your trust in God;*
for I will yet give thanks to him,
who is the help of my counte - / nance, and my God.

4 LENT A

REFRAIN

The Lord is my shep-herd; I shall not be in want.

PSALM 23   TONE VI

2 *He mäkes* me lie down in / green pás-tures*
     and leads me be - / side ẗill wa-ters.
3 He / re-víves my soul*
     and guides me along right pathways / for his
                              Näme's sake.

                              REFRAIN

4a *Though Ï* walk through the valley of the
                              sha - / dow óf death,*
      I shall / fear nö é-vil;
4b For you / are wíth me;*
      your rod and your / staff, thëy cóm-fort me.

                              REFRAIN

5 *You sprëad* a table before me in the presence of
                              those / who tróu-ble me;*
     you have anointed my head with oil,
     and my cup is / run-niṅg ó-ver.
6 Surely your goodness and mercy shall follow me
                              all the days / of mý life,*
     and I will dwell in the house of the / LORD för év-er.

                              REFRAIN

BCP, p. 612

4 LENT A

TONE II

VERSE (John 8:12)

I am the light of the world, says the LORD;*
whoever follows me will have / the light of life.

OR

TRACT (Psalm 122)

1 *I was* glad when they said to me,*
   "Let us go to the house / of the LORD."

2 Now our feet are stand-ing*
   within your gates, O / Je-ru-sa-lem.

3 Jerusalem is built as a cit-y*
   that is at uni - / ty with it-self;

4 To which the tribes go up,
   the tribes of the LORD,*
      the assembly of Israel,
      to praise the Name / of the LORD.

5 For there are the thrones of judg-ment,*
      the thrones of the house / of Da-vid.

6 Pray for the peace of Je-ru-sa-lem:*
   "May they prosper / who love you.

7 Peace be within your walls*
   and quietness within / your tow-ers.

8 For my brethren and com-pan-ions' sake,*
   I pray for your / pros-per-i-ty.

9 Because of the house of the LORD our God,*
   I will seek / to do you good."   *BCP, p. 779*

5 LENT A

REFRAIN

With the Lord there is mer-cy; with him there

is   plen-te-ous re - demp - tion.

PSALM 130   TONE III*b*

1 *Out of* the depths have I called to you, O LORD;
   LORD, hear my voice;*
        let your ears consider well the voice of
                      my sup - / pli-ca-tion.

                                    REFRAIN

2 *If you*, LORD, were to note what is done a-miss,*
      O LORD, / who could stand?
3 For there is for-give-ness with you;*
      therefore / you shall be feared.

                                    REFRAIN

4 *I wait* for the LORD; my soul waits for him;*
      in his word / is my hope.
5 My soul waits for the LORD,
   more than watchmen for the morn-ing,*
      more than watchmen for / the morn-ing.

                                    REFRAIN

6 *O Is* - rael, wait for the LORD,*
      for with the LORD there / is mer-cy;
7 With him there is plente-ous re-demp-tion,*
      and he shall redeem Israel / from all their sins.

                                    REFRAIN
                                    BCP, p. 784

5 LENT A

TONE II

VERSE (John 11:25,26)

I am the resurrection and the life, says the Lord;*
whoever believes in me shall not die / for év-er.

OR

TRACT (Psalm 129)

1 *"Great - ly* have they oppressed me since my youth,"*
   let Is - / ra-él now say;

2 "Greatly have they oppressed me since my youth,*
   but they have not prevailed / a-gáinst me."

3 The plowmen plowed up-ón my back*
   and made / their fúr-rows long.

4 The LORD, the Right-eous One,*
   has cut the cords of / the wick-ed.

5 Let them be put to shame and thrówn back,*
   all those who are enemies / of Zí-on.

6 Let them be like grass upon the house-tops,*
   which withers before / it cán be plucked;

7 Which does not fill the hand of the reap-er,*
   nor the bosom of him / who binds the sheaves;

8 So that those who go by say not so much as,
   "The LORD prós-per you.*
   We wish you well in the Name / of thé LORD."

During the procession, all hold branches in their hands and appropriate hymns, psalms, or anthems are sung, such as the hymn "All glory, laud and honor," and the following Psalm:

ANTIPHON

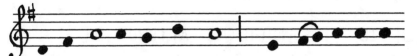

Ho-san-na in the high-est. Bless-ed is he who

comes in the name of the Lord.

(REFRAIN)

Ho-san-na in the high-est. *

(* The italicized portion of the Antiphon is to be repeated as a Refrain after each verse of the Psalm.

PSALM 118   ANCIENT GALLICAN CHANT

19 *O - pen* for me the gates of righteousness;*
    I will enter them;
    I will offer thanks to / the LŎRD.   *Refrain*

20 *"This is* the gate of the LORD;*
    he who is righteous / may én-ter."   *Refrain*

(continued)

REFRAIN

Ho-san-na in the high-est.

PSALM 118 ANCIENT GALLICAN CHANT

21 *I will* give thanks to you, for you answered me*
and have become my / sal-vá-tion. *Refrain*

22 *The same* stone which the builders rejected*
has become the / chief cór-ner-stone. *Refrain*

23 *This is* the LORD'S doing,*
and it is marve - / lous in our eyes. *Refrain*

24 *On this* day the LORD has acted;*
we will rejoice and / be glád in it. *Refrain*

25 *Ho - san -* nah, LORD, hosannah!*
LORD, send / us now suc-cess. *Refrain*

26 *Bless - ed* is he who comes in the name of the Lord;*
we bless you from the house of / the LÖRD.

Refrain

27 *God is* the LORD; he has shined upon us;*
form a procession with branches up to
the horns of / the ál-tar.

Refrain

(continued)

REFRAIN

Ho-san-na in the high-est.

PSALM 118   ANCIENT GALLICAN CHANT

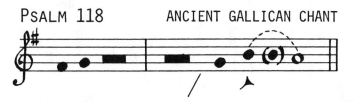

28 *"You are* my God, and I will thank you;*
   you are my God, and I will / ex-ált you."

Refrain

29 *Give thanks* to the LORD, for he is good;*
   his mercy endures / for év-er.   *Refrain*

THE COMPLETE ANTIPHON
MAY THEN BE REPEATED.

=========

This Psalm is taken from *Music for Ministers and Congregation* (The Church Hymnal Corporation, ©1978), and is used by permission in this Psalm Collection. Additional music for the Sunday of the Passion can be found in *Music for Ministers and Congregation,* pages 28-31.

PASSION (PALM) SUNDAY A

At the Procession:

REFRAIN

Ho - san - na in the high-est.

PSALM 118 TONE VIIa

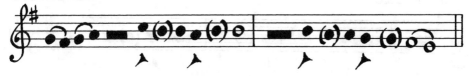

19 Ö - *pën* for me the gátes of ríght-eous-ness;*
    I will enter them;
    I will offer thánks to thé LORD.

REFRAIN

20 "*Thïs ïs* the gáte of thé LORD;*
    he who is ríght-eous may én-tër."

REFRAIN

21 *I wïll* give thanks to you, fór you án-swered me*
    and have be-cöme my sal-vä-tiön.

REFRAIN

22 *The säme* stone which the búild-ers re-jéct-ed*
    has be-cöme the chief cór-ner-stöne.

REFRAIN

23 —— This ís the LORD'S dó-ing,*
    and it is már-vel-ous ín our ëyes.

REFRAIN

24 *Ön thïs* day the LÓRD has áct-ed;*
    we will re-jóice and be glád in ít.

REFRAIN

(continued) *BCP, p. 762*

At the Procession:

REFRAIN

Ho-san-na in the high-est.

PSALM 118   TONE VIIa

25 *Hö - sän* - nah, LORD, ho-sán-nah!*
   LORD, sénd us nów suc-cess.

REFRAIN

26 *Bless - ed* is he who comes in the náme of thé Lord;*
   we bless you from the house of thé LORD.

REFRAIN

27 *Göd is* the LORD; he has shined up-ón us;*
   form a procession with branches up to
                    the horns of the ál-tär.

REFRAIN

28 *"Yöu are* my God, and Í will thánk you;*
   you are my God, and Í will ex-ált yöu."

REFRAIN

29 *Give thanks* to the LORD, for hé is good;*
   his mercy en-dúres for év-eör.

REFRAIN

At the Eucharist:

REFRAIN

My God, my God, why have you for-sak-en me?

PSALM 22   **TONE IV***e*

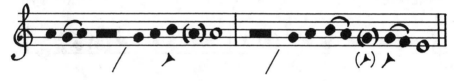

1 *My God,* my God, why have / you for-sák-en me?*
      and are so far from my cry
      and from / the words öf mÿ dis-tress?
2 O my God, I cry in the daytime, but you / do
                     ₁not án-swer;*
      by night as well, / but I find ñö rest.
3 Yet you / are the Hó-ly One,*
      enthroned upon the / prais-es öf Iś-r̈a-el.

                                    REFRAIN

4 *Our fore* - fathers / put their trúst in you;*
      they trusted, / and you dë-lív-er̈ed them.
5 They cried out to you and / were de-lív-ered;*
      they trusted in you / and were nöt pút tö shame.
6 But as for me, I am a / worm and ñó man,*
      scorned by all and de - / spised by thë p̈eö-ple.

                                    REFRAIN

7 *All who* see me laugh / me to scórn;*
      they curl their lips and / wag their heäds, säy-ing,
8 "He trusted in the LORD; let / him de-lív-er him;*
      let him rescue him, / if he dë-lights iñ him."
9 Yet you are he who took me out / of the womb,*
      and kept me safe / up-on mÿ móth-er̈'s breast.

                                    REFRAIN

(continued)   *BCP, p. 610*

At the Eucharist:

REFRAIN

My God, my God, why have you for-sak-en me?

PSALM 22   **TONE IV*e***

10 *I häve* been entrusted to you ev - / er since Í was born;*
     you were my God when I was / still in mÿ
                    móth-ër's womb.
11 Be not far from me, for trou - / ble is neár,*
     —— / and there iš nóne tö help.

                                REFRAIN

BCP, p. 610

PASSION (PALM) SUNDAY A

TONE II

VERSE (Phil. 2:8,9)

Christ for us became obedient unto death, even
death on a cróss;*
therefore God has highly exalted him
and bestowed on him the name which is a - / bove
éve-ry name.

OR

TRACT (Psalm 22)

26 *All the* ends of the earth shall remember and turn to
the LÓRD,*
and all the families of the nations shall
bow / be-fóre him.

27 For kingship belongs to the LÓRD;*
he rules over / the ná-tions.

28 To him alone all who sleep in the earth bow down
in wór-ship;*
all who go down to the dust fall / be-fóre him.

29 My soul shall live for him;
my descendants shall sérve him;*
they shall be known as the LORD'S / for év-er.

30 They shall come and make known to a people yét un-born*
the saving deeds / that hé has done.

MONDAY IN HOLY WEEK ABC

REFRAIN

In your light, O God, we see light.

PSALM 36   TONE I_g

5 *Your löve*, O LORD, reaches tó the héav-ens,*
   and your faith - / ful-ness to the clouds.
6 Your righteousness is like the strong mountains,
   your justice líke the gréat deep;*
   you save both / man and beäst, O LORD.

                           REFRAIN

7 *How príce* - less ís your lóve, O God!*
   your people take refuge under the
                   sha - / dow of yöur wings.
8 They feast upon the a-bún-dance óf your house;*
   you give them drink from the ri - / ver of
                   yöur de-lights.

                           REFRAIN

9 *For with* you ís the wéll of life,*
   and in your / light we säe light.
10 Continue your loving-kindness to thóse who knów you,*
   and your favor to those / who are trüe of heart.

                           REFRAIN

Monday in Holy Week ABC

Tone II

Verse

We *a* - dore you, O Christ, and we bléss you,*
because by your holy cross you have / re-deémed
the world.

OR

Tract   (Psalm 102)

1 LORD, *hear* my prayer, and let my cry come be-fóre you;*
   hide not your face from me in the day of / my tróu-ble.

2 Incline your eár to me;*
   when I call, make haste / to án-swer me,

3 For my days drift away like smóke,*
   and my bones are hot / as búrn-ing coals.

4 My heart is smitten like grass and wíth-ered,*
   so that I forget / to eát my bread.

12 But you, O LORD, endure for év-er,*
    and your Name / from aǵe to age.

13 You will arise and have compassion on Zion,
    for it is time to have mercy up-ón her;*
    indeed, the appoint - / ed tíme has come.

REFRAIN

I have tak-en re-fuge in you, O Lord.

PSALM 71   TONE II

2 *In your* righteousness, deliver me and sét me free;*
   incline your ear to me / and sáve me.
3 Be my strong rock, a castle to keép me safe;*
   you are my crag and / my stróng-hold.

                                      REFRAIN

4 *De - liv -* er me, my God, from the hand of the wíck-ed,*
   from the clutches of the evildoer and
                       the / op-prés-sor.
10 For my enemies are talking a-gáinst me,*
   and those who lie in wait for my life take
                 counsel / to-géth-er.

                                        REFRAIN

11 *They say,* "God has forsaken him;
   go after him and séize him;*
   because there is none / who wíll save."
12 O God, be not fár from me;*
   come quickly to help / me, Ó my God.

                                        REFRAIN

VERSE OR TRACT AS ON MONDAY   *BCP, p. 683*

WEDNESDAY IN HOLY WEEK ABC

REFRAIN

An-swer me, O God, in your great mer-cy.

PSALM 69   TONE III*a*

7 *Let nöt* those who hope in you be put to shame through mé,
        Lord GÓD öf hosts;*
    let not those who seek you be disgraced because of me,
        O God / of Iś-ra-ël.
8 Surely, for your sake have I súf-fered rë-proach,*
    and shame has cov - / ered mý fáce.

REFRAIN

9 *I häve* become a stranger to mý own kín-dred,*
    an alien to my moth - / er's chíl-drën.
10 Zeal for your house has eát-en më up;*
    the scorn of those who scorn you has fallen / up-ón më.

REFRAIN

14 *But äs* for me, thís is my práyer tö you,*
    at the time you / have sét, O LORD:
15 "In your great mér-cy, Ö God,*
    answer me with your / un-fáil-ing hëlp."

REFRAIN

22 *Re - pröach* has broken my heart, and it cán-not bë healed;*
    I looked for sympathy, but there was none,
    for comforters, but I could / find nó ońe.
23 They gáve me gáll tö eat,*
    and when I was thirsty, they gave me vine - / gar tó
        drïnk.

REFRAIN

VERSE OR TRACT AS ON MONDAY

BCP, p. 679

Maundy Thursday ABC

REFRAIN

Mor-tals ate the bread of an-gels,

for the Lord gave them man - na from heav-en.

PSALM 78   **TONE V**$_a$

14 *He led* them with a cloud by day,*
    and all the night through with a glow of fire.
14 He split the hard rocks in the wil-der-ness*
    and gave them drink as from the great deep.

                           REFRAIN

17 *But they* went on sinning a-gainst him,*
    rebelling in the desert a-gainst the Most High.
18 They tested God in their hearts,*
    demanding food for their crav-ing.

                           REFRAIN

19 *They railed* against God and said,*
    "Can God set a table in the wil-der-ness?"
23 So he commanded the clouds above*
    and opened the doors of heav-en.

                           REFRAIN

24 *He rained* down manna upon them to eat*
    and gave them grain from heav-en.
25 So mortals ate the bread of an-gels;*
    he provided for them food e-nough.

                           REFRAIN
BCP, p. 696

Maundy Thursday ABC

VERSE   (John 13:34)

> A *new* commandment I gíve to you:*
>   love one another as / I have lovéd you.

OR

TRACT   (Psalm 43)

1 *Give judg* - ment for me, O God,
     and defend my cause against an ungodly péo-ple;*
          deliver me from the deceitful / and the wíck-ed.

2 For you are the God of my strength;
     why have you put me fróm you?*
          and why do I go so heavily while the ene - / my
                    op-préss-es me?

3 Send out your light and your truth, that they
                    may leád me,*
          and bring me to your holy hill
          and / to your dwéll-ing;

4 That I may go to the altar of God,
     to the God of my joy and glád-ness;*
          and on the harp I will give thanks to / you,
                    O Gód my God.

5 Why are you so full of heaviness, Ó my soul?*
          and why are you so disquiet - / ed with-ín me?

6 Put your trúst in God;*
          for I will yet give thanks to him,
          who is the help of my coun - / te-nance, and my .God.

GOOD FRIDAY ABC

REFRAIN

My God, my God, why have you for-sak-en me?

PSALM 22   TONE IVe

1 *My God,* my God, why have / you for-sák-en me?*
   and are so far from my cry
   and from / the words öf mÿ dis-tress?
2 O my God, I cry in the daytime, but you / do not
                     an-swer;*
   by night as well, / but I find ñö rest.

                          REFRAIN

7 *All who* see me laugh / me to scórn;*
   they curl their lips and / wag their heäds, säy-ing,
8 "He trusted in the LORD; let / him de-lív-er him;*
   let him rescue him, / if he dë-ligñts iñ him."

                          REFRAIN

14 *I am* poured out like water;
    all my / bones are oút of joint;*
    my heart within / my breast iÿ mélt-iñg wax.
15 My mouth is dried out like a pot-sherd;
    my tongue sticks to the roof / of my moúth;*
    and you have laid me / in the düst öf thë grave.

                          REFRAIN

(continued)   *BCP, p. 610*

GOOD FRIDAY ABC *(continuation)*

REFRAIN

My God, my God, why have you for - sak-en me?

PSALM 22   **TONE IV***e*

16 *Packs öf* dogs close me in,
     and gangs of evildoers cir - / cle a-roúnd me;*
        they pierce my hands and my feet;
        / I can coünt áll mÿ bones.
17 They stare and gloat / o-ver mé;*
        they divide my garments among them;
        they cast / lots for mÿ clöth-ing.

                                              REFRAIN

18 *Be nöt* —— / far a-wáy, O LORD;*
        you are my strength; / has-ten tö hélp me.
19 Save me / from the swórd,*
        my life from / the pow-ër óf thë dog.

                                              REFRAIN

20 *Save mё* —— / from the lí-on's mouth,*
        my wretched body / from the hoŕns óf ẅild bulls.
21 I will declare your Name / to my bréth-ren;*
        in the midst of the congrega - / tion I ẅill
                              pŕaise you.

                                              REFRAIN

BCP, p. 610

Good Friday ABC

Tone II

Verse (Phil. 2:8,9)

> *Christ for* us became obedient unto death,
> even death on a cróss;*
>   therefore God has highly exalted him
>   and bestowed on him the name which is a - / bove
>   eve-ry name.

OR

Tract (Psalm 40)

1 *I wait* - ed patiently up-ón the LORD;*
    he stooped to me / and heárd my cry.

2 He lifted me out of the desolate pit,
                    out of the míre and clay;*
    he set my feet upon a high cliff
                    and made / my fóot-ing sure.

3 He put a new song in my mouth,
    a song of praise to our Gód;*
        many shall see, and stand in awe,
        and put their trust / in thé LORD.

4 Happy are they who trust in the LÓRD!*
        they do not resort to evil spirits
                        or turn / to fálse gods.

5 Great things are they that you have done, O LORD my God!
    how great your wonders and your pláns for us!*
        there is none who can be / com-páred with you.

6 Oh, that I could make them known and téll them!*
        but they are more / than Í can count.

(continued)   *BCP, p. 640*

Tone II

7 In sacrifice and offering you take no pléas-ure*
   (you have given me ears / to héar you);

8 Burnt-offering and sin-offering you have nót re-quired,*
   and so I said, / "Be-hóld, I come.

9 In the roll of the book it is written con-cérn-ing me:*
   'I love to do your will, O my God;
   your law is deep / in mý heart.'"

10 I proclaimed righteousness in the great con-gre-gá-tion;*
    behold, I did not restrain my lips;
    and that, / O LÓRD, you know.

11 Your righteousness have I not hidden in my heart;
    I have spoken of your faithfulness and your
                            de-lív-er-ance;*
    I have not concealed your love and faithfulness
                            from the great con - / gre-gá-tion.

12 You are the LORD;
    do not withhold your compassion fróm me;*
    let your love and your faithfulness keep
                    me safe / for év-er,

13 For innumerable troubles have crowded upon me;
    my sins have overtaken me, and I cán-not see;*
    they are more in number than the hairs of my head,
    and my / heart fáils me.

14 Be pleased, O LORD, to de-lív-er me;*
    O LORD, make haste / to hélp me.

TONE II

VERSE   (Phil. 2:8,9)

Christ for us became obedient unto death,
even death on a cróss;*
     therefore God has highly exalted him
     and bestowed on him the name which is a - / bove
               eve-ry name.

OR

TRACT   (Psalm 69)

1 —— Save me, O Gód,*
     for the waters have risen up / to mý neck.

2 I am sinking in déep mire,*
     and there is no firm ground / for mý feet.

3 I have come into deep wá-ters,*
     and the torrent wash - / es ó-ver me.

4 I have grown weary with my crying;
   my throat is in-flámed;*
     my eyes have failed from look - / ing fór my God.

5 Those who hate me without a cause are more than
                    the hairs of my head;
   my lying foes who would destroy me are míght-y.*
     Must I then give back what / I név-er stole?

6 O God, you know my fóol-ish-ness,*
     and my faults are not hid - / den fróm you.

7 Let not those who hope in you be put to shame through me,
                    Lord GÓD of hosts;*
     let not those who seek you be disgraced because of me,
                    O God / of Iś-ra-el.

(continued)   *BCP, p. 679*

TONE II

8   Surely, for your sake have I suffered re-próach,*
     and shame has cov - / ered mý face.

9   I have become a stranger to my own kín-dred,*
     an alien to my moth - / er's chíl-dren.

10 Zeal for your house has eaten me úp;*
     the scorn of those who scorn you has fallen / up-ón me.

14 But as for me, this is my práyer to you,*
     at the time you / have sét, O LORD:

15 "In your great mercy, O Gód,*
     answer me with your / un-fáil-ing help.

16 Save me from the mire; do not let me sínk;*
     let me be rescued from those who hate me
     and out of the / deep wá-ters.

17 Let not the torrent of waters wash over me,
     neither let the deep swallow me úp;*
     do not let the Pit shut its mouth / up-ón me.

18 Answer me, O LORD, for your lóve is kind;*
     in your great compas - / sion, túrn to me."

19 "Hide not your face from your sér-vant;*
     be swift and answer me, for I / am ín dis-tress.

20 Draw near to me and re-deém me;*
     because of my enemies / de-lív-er me.

21 You know my reproach, my shame, and my dis-hón-or;*
     my adversaries are all / in yóur sight."

(continued)   BCP, p. 679

TONE II

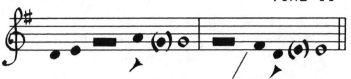

22 Reproach has broken my heart, and it cannot be héaled;*
    I looked for sympathy, but there was none,
    for comforters, but I could / find nó one.

23 They gave me gáll to eat,*
        and when I was thirsty, they gave me vin - / e-gár
                        to drink.

REFRAIN

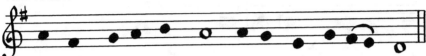

Fa-ther, in-to your hands I com-mend my spir-it.

PSALM 31   TONE VIIb

1 *In you,* O LORD, have I taken refuge;
     let me név-er be pút to shame;*
        delíver me iń your ríght-eous-ness.
2 In-clíne your eár to me;*
     make háste to de-lív-er me.

                                    REFRAIN

3 *Be my* strong rock, a castle to keep me safe,
     for you are my crág and my stróng-hold;*
        for the sake of your Name, leád me and gúide me.
4 Take me out of the net that they have sé-cret-ly
                   sét for me,*
     for you are my tów-er óf strength.

                                    REFRAIN

5 *In-to* your hands I com-ménd my spír-it,*
     for you have redeemed me,
        O LÓRD, O Gód of truth.
16 Make your face to shine up-oń your sér-vant,*
     and in your loving-kińd-ness sáve me.

                                    REFRAIN

BCP, p. 622

Holy Saturday ABC

Verse

We a-dore you, O Christ, and we bléss you,*
   because by your holy cross you have / re-deémed
        the world.

OR

Tract   (Psalm 130)

1 *Out of* the depths have I called to you, O LORD;
  LORD, heár my voice;*
    let your ears consider well the voice of
               my sup - / pli-cá-tion.

2 If you, LORD, were to note what is dóne a-miss,*
  O Lord, / who coúld stand?

3 For there is forgiveness with yóu;*
  therefore / you sháll be feared.

4 I wait for the LORD; my şoul ẃaits for him;*
  in his word / is mý hope.

5 My soul waits for the LORD,
  more than watchmen for the mórn-ing,*
    more than watchmen for / the mórn-ing.

6 O Israel, wait for the LÓRD,*
  for with the LORD there / is mér-cy;

7 With him there is plenteous re-démp-tion,*
  and he shall redeem Israel / from áll their sins.

BCP, p. 784

Easter Vigil ABC

Refrain

By the word of the Lord were the heav-ens made,

by the breath of his mouth all the heav-en-ly hosts.

Psalm 33　　　　　　　　　　　Tone I f

1 *Re - joïce* in the LÓRD, you ríght-eous;*
    it is good for the just / to sing práis-ës.
2 Praise the LÓRD with thé harp;*
    play to him upon the / psal-ter-ÿ and lÿre.

REFRAIN

3 *Sing för* —— hím a néw song;*
    sound a fanfare with all your skill up - / on
                the trüm-pët.
4 For the wórd of the LÓRD is right,*
    and / all his wórks are süre.

REFRAIN

5 *He loves* right-eous-néss and júdg-ment;*
    the loving-kindness of the LORD / fills the
                whöle eärth.
7 He gathers up the waters of the ocean as ín a
                wá-ter-skin*
    and stores up the / depths of thé sëa.

REFRAIN

(continued)

REFRAIN

By the word of the Lord were the heav-ens made,

by the breath of his mouth all the heav-en-ly hosts.

PSALM 33   TONE I*f*

8 *Let all* the earth fear thé LORD;*
   let all who dwell in the world / stand in awe of him.
9 For he spóke, and it cáme to pass;*
   he commanded, / and it stóöd fäst.

REFRAIN

10 *The LORD* brings the will of the ná-tions tó naught;*
    he thwarts the designs / of the péö-plës.
11 But the LORD'S will stands fást for év-er,*
    and the designs of his / heart from áge to äge.

REFRAIN

Easter Vigil ABC

Refrain

In your light, O God, we see light.

Psalm 36   Tone VI

5 *Your löve*, O LORD, reaches to / the héav-ens,*
   and your faith - / ful-nëss tó the clouds.
6 Your righteousness is like the strong mountains,
   your justice like / the gréat deep;*
   you save both / man aṅd beást, O LORD.

REFRAIN

7 *How prïce* - less is / your lóve, O God!*
   your people take refuge under the
                  sha - / dow öf yóur wings.
8 They feast upon the abun - / dance óf your house;*
   you give them drink from the riv - / er öf yóur
                  de-lights.

REFRAIN

9 *For wïth* you is / the wéll of life,*
   and in your / light wë sée light.
10 Continue your loving-kindness to those / who knów you,*
   and your favor to those / who aïe trúe of heart.

REFRAIN

EASTER VIGIL ABC

REFRAIN

The Lord of hosts is with us;

the God of Ja - cob is our strong-hold.

PSALM 46   TONE VIIIg

1 *God is* our refuge and stréngth,*
   a very present / help in tróu-ble.
2 Therefore we will not fear, though the eárth be moved,*
   and though the mountains be toppled into
              the / depths of thé sea.
3 Though its waters ráge and foam,*
   and though the mountains tremble / at its tú-mult.

                              REFRAIN

5 *There is* a river whose streams make glad the
                 city of Gód,*
   the holy habitation / of the Móst High.
6 God is in the midst of her;
   she shall not be ó-ver-thrown;*
   God shall help her / at the bréak of day.
7 The nations make much ado, and the kingdoms
                are shák-en;*
   God has spoken, and the / earth shall mélt a-way.

                              REFRAIN

(continued)   *BCP, p. 649*

REFRAIN

The Lord of hosts is with us;

the God   of Ja - cob is our   strong-hold.

PSALM 46   TONE VIII*g*

9 *Come now* and look upon the works of the LORD,*
      what awesome things / he has done on earth.
10 It is he who makes war to cease in áll the world;*
      he breaks the bow, and shatters the spear,
      and / burns the shiélds with fire.
11 "Be still, then, and know that Í am God;*
      I will be exalted among the nations;
      I will be ex - / alt-ed iń the earth."

                              REFRAIN

BCP, p. 649

Easter Vigil ABC

Refrain

Hap-py is the na-tion whose God is the Lord.

Psalm 33 — Tone VI

13 *The LÖRD* looks down / from héav-en,*
    and beholds all the / peo-plë iñ the world.
14 From where he sits enthroned / he túrns his gaze*
    on all / who dwëll ón the earth.
15 He fashions all / the héarts of them*
    and un - / der-stäñds áll their works.

REFRAIN

16 *There ïs* no king that can be saved by a might - / y
    ár-my;*
    a strong man is not delivered / by hïs gréat strength
18 Behold, the eye of the LORD is upon those / who
    féar him,*
    on those who wait / up-öñ hís love,
19 To pluck / their líves from death,*
    and to feed them in / time öf fám-ine.

REFRAIN

20 *Our söul* waits / for thé LORD;*
    he is our / help añd oúr shield.
21 Indeed, our heart rejoic - / es iñ him,*
    for in his holy / Name wë pút our trust.
22 Let your loving-kindness, O LORD, be / up-öñ us,*
    as we have / put oür trúst in you.

REFRAIN

BCP, p. 627

Easter Vigil ABC

Refrain

Pro-tect me, O God, for I take ref-uge in you.

Psalm 16   Tone VI

5 *O LORD*, you are my por - / tion and my cup;*
   it is you / who up-hold my lot.
6 My boundaries enclose / a pleas-ant land;*
   indeed, I have a / good-ly her-i-tage.

                                    REFRAIN

8 *I have* set the LORD always / be-fore me;*
   because he is at my right / hand I shall not fall.
9 My heart, therefore, is glad, and my spirit / re-joic-es;*
   my body al - / so shall rest in hope.

                                    REFRAIN

10 *For you* will not abandon / me to the grave,*
   nor let your ho - / ly one see the Pit.
11 You will show me / the path of life;*
   in your presence there is fullness of joy,
   and in your right hand are pleas - / ures for
          ev-er-more.

                                    REFRAIN

EASTER VIGIL ABC

REFRAIN

I will sing to the Lord,

for he has ris-en up in might.

CANTICLE 8   TONE VIII*g*

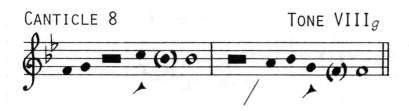

1 *I will* sing to the Lord, for he is lofty and up-líft-ed;*
  the horse and its rider has he / hurled in-tó the sea.
2 The Lord is my strength and my réf-uge;*
  the Lord has be - / come my Sáv-ior.

REFRAIN

3 *This is* my God and I will práise him,*
  the God of my people and I / will ex-ált him.
4 The Lord is a mighty wár-rior;*
  —— / Yah-weh ís his Name.

REFRAIN

5 *The char* - iots of Pharaoh and his army has he
            hurled into the séa;*
  the finest of those who bear armor have been
            drowned / in the Réd Sea.
6 The fathomless deep has over-whélmed them;*
  they sank into the / depths like á stone.

REFRAIN

(continued)

EASTER VIGIL ABC   *(continuation)*

REFRAIN

I will sing to the Lord,

for he has ris-en up in might.

CANTICLE 8   TONE VIII*g*

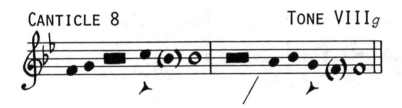

7 *Your right* hand, O Lord, is glorious in might;*
    your right hand, O Lord, has over - / thrown
                the en-e-my.
8 Who can be compared with you, O Lord, among the gods?*
    who is like you, glorious in holiness,
    awesome in renown, and work - / er of won-ders?

                          REFRAIN

9 *You stretched* forth your right hand;*
    the earth / swal-lowed them up.
10 With your constant love you led the people you re-deemed;*
    with your might you brought them in safety to
                your / ho-ly dwell-ing.

                          REFRAIN

11 *You will* bring them in and plant them*
    on the mount of / your pos-ses-sion,
12 The resting-place you have made for your-self, O Lord,*
    the sanctuary, O Lord, that your hand / has
                es-tab-lished.
13 The Lord shall reign*
    for ev - / er and ev-er.

                          REFRAIN

BCP, p. 85

EASTER VIGIL ABC

REFRAIN

Pray for the peace of Je-ru-sa-lem.

PSALM 122   TONE VI

1 *I wäs* glad when / they s̈aid to me,*
   "Let us go to / the hoüse öf the LORD."
2 Now our feet / are stánd-ing*
   within your gates, / O Jë-rú-sa-lem.
                                    REFRAIN

3 *Je - r̈u* - sa-lem is built as / a ćit-y*
   that is at u - / ni-tÿ ẃith it-self;
4 To which the tribes go up,
   the tribes of / the LÓRD,*
   the assembly of Israel,
   to praise / the Naᵐe öf the LORD.
                                    REFRAIN

6 *Pray för* the peace of / Je-rú-sa-lem:*
   "May they pros - / per whö lóve you.
7 Peace be / with-iń your walls*
   and quietness with - / in yöur tów-ers.
                                    REFRAIN

8 *For m̈y* brethren and / com-pán-ions' sake,*
   I pray for / your prös-pér-i-ṭy.
9 Because of the house of / the LÓRD our God,*
   I will / seek tö dó you good."
                                    REFRAIN

BCP, p. 779

Easter Vigil ABC

Refrain

You shall draw wa-ter with re - joic-ing

from the springs of sal-va - tion.

Canticle 9   Tone VIIIg

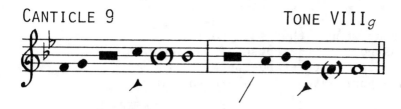

1 *Sure - ly*, it is God who saves me;*
   I will trust in him and / not be á-fraid.
2 For the Lord is my stronghold and my súre de-fense,*
   and he will / be my Sáv-ior.

REFRAIN

4 *And on* that day you shall sáy,*
   Give thanks to the Lord and / call up-ón his Name;
5 Make his deeds known among the péo-ples;*
   see that they remember that his Name / is ex-ált-ed.

REFRAIN

6 *Sing the* praises of the Lord, for he has done
                    gréat things,*
   and this is / known in áll the world.
7 Cry aloud, inhabitants of Zion, ring out your jóy,*
   for the great one in the midst of you is
                    the Holy / One of Iś-ra-el.

REFRAIN

BCP, p. 86

Easter Vigil ABC

REFRAIN

As the deer longs for the wa-ter-brooks,

so longs my soul for you, O God.

PSALM 42   TONE VIII*g*

2 *My soul* is athirst for God, athirst for the
            lív-ing God;*
    when shall I come to appear before the / pres-ence
            óf God?
3 My tears have been my food dáy and night,*
    while all day long they say to me,
    / "Where is nów your God?"

                                    REFRAIN

4 *I pour* out my soul when I think on these thíngs:*
    how I went with the multitude and led them
            in - / to the hoúse of God,
5 With the voice of praise and thánks-giv-ing,*
    among those / who keep hó-ly-day.

                                    REFRAIN

6 *Why are* you so full of heaviness, Ó my soul?*
    and why are you so disquiet - / ed with-ín me?
7 Put your trust in Gód;*
    for I will yet give thanks to him,
    who is the help of my coun - / te-nance, añd my God.

                                    REFRAIN

EASTER VIGIL ABC

REFRAIN

You brought me up, O Lord, from the dead.

PSALM 30   **TONE VI**

1 *I will* exalt you, O LORD,
   because you have lifted / me up*
      and have not let my enemies / tri-umph o-ver me.
2 O LORD my God, I / cried out to you,*
   and you / re-stored me to health.
3 You brought me up, O LORD, from / the dead;*
   you restored my life as I was go - / ing down to
                          the grave.
                                              REFRAIN

4 *Sing to* the LORD, you servants / of his;*
   give thanks for the remembrance / of his ho-li-ness.
5 For his wrath endures but the twinkling of / an eye,*
   his favor / for a life-time.
6 Weeping may spend / the night,*
   but joy comes / in the morn-ing.
                                              REFRAIN

12 *You have* turned my wailing in - / to danc-ing;*
    you have put off my sack-cloth / and clothed' me
                           with joy.
13 Therefore my heart sings to you with - / out ceas-ing;*
    O LORD my God, I will give you / thanks for ev-er.
                                              REFRAIN

BCP, p. 621

EASTER VIGIL ABC

REFRAIN

Re-vive me, O Lord, for your Name's sake.

PSALM 143   TONE VI

1   *LORD, hear* my prayer,
   and in your faithfulness heed my sup - / pli-ca-tions;*
     answer me / in your right-eous-ness.
2   Enter not into judgment with / your sér-vant,*
     for in your sight shall no one liv -/ ing bë jús-ti-fied.

REFRAIN

4   *My spir -* it faints / with-in me;*
     my heart within / me is dés-o-late.
5   I remember the time past;
   I muse up - / on áll your deeds;*
     I consider / the works óf your hands.

REFRAIN

6   *I spread* out / my hánds to you;*
     my soul gasps to you / like a thírst-y land.
7   O LORD, make haste to answer me; my spir - / it fáils me;*
   do not hide your face from me
     or I shall be like those who / go down tó the Pit.

REFRAIN

8   *Let me* hear of your loving-kindness in the morning,
   for I put / my trúst in you;*
     show me the road that I must walk,
     for I lift / up mÿ sóul to you.
10   Teach me to do what pleases you, for you / are mÿ God;*
     let your good Spirit lead / me on lév-el ground.

REFRAIN

DCT, p. 798

REFRAIN

Shout with joy to the Lord, all you lands;

lift up your voice, re-joice, and sing.

PSALM 98   TONE VIIIc

1 *Sing to* the LORD a néw song,*
    for he / has done már-ve̲l̲o̲u̲s things.
2 With his right hand and his hó-ly arm*
    has he won for him - / self the víc-to-ry.

REFRAIN

3 *The LORD* has made known his víc-to-ry;*
    his righteousness has he openly shown in
               the sight / of the ná-tions.
4 He remembers his mercy and faithfulness to
               the house of Is̲-ra-el,*
    and all the ends of the earth have seen the
               vic - / to-ry óf our God.

REFRAIN

6 *Sing to* the LORD with the hárp,*
    with the harp / and the vóice of song.
7 With trumpets and the sound of the hórn*
    shout with joy be - / fore the Kíng, the LORD.

REFRAIN

(continued)

REFRAIN

Shout with joy to the Lord, all   you lands;

lift up your voice, re-joice, and sing.

PSALM 98   TONE VIIIc

8 *Let the* sea make a noise and all that is ín it,*
   the lands and / those who dwéll there-in.
9 Let the rivers cláp their hands,*
   and let the hills ring out with joy before the LORD,
   when he / comes to júdge the earth.

REFRAIN

REFRAIN

The Lord has done great things for us,

and we are glad in-deed.

PSALM 126   TONE VIII*g*

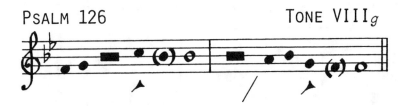

1   *When the* LORD restored the fortunes of Zí-on,*
        then were / we like thóse who dream.
2   Then was our mouth filled with laúgh-ter,*
        and our / tongue with shóuts of joy.

                                              REFRAIN

3   *Then they* said among the ná-tions,*
        "The LORD has / done great thíngs for them."
4   The LORD has done great thíngs for us,*
        and / we are glád in-deed.

                                              REFRAIN

5   *Re - store* our fortunes, O LÓRD,*
        like the watercourses / of the Né-gev.
6   Those who sowed with teárs*
        will / reap with sóngs of joy.

                                              REFRAIN

7   *Those who* go out weeping, carrying the seéd,*
        will come again with joy, shoul - / der-ing
                    théir sheaves.

                                              REFRAIN

EASTER DAY ABC - *At an Early Service*

One of the Old Testament lessons from the Great Vigil of Easter is used, followed by the corresponding Psalm or Canticle.

THE GREAT ALLELUIA

After the Epistle, this Alleluia is traditionally sung three times by the Celebrant or by a Cantor, at successively higher pitches, the Congregation repeating it each time.

V.&R. Al - le - - - lu - - ia.

V.&R. Al - le - - - lu - - ia.

V.&R. Al - le - - - lu - - ia.

Followed by:

REFRAIN ALLELUIA VII

Hal-le-lu - jah, hal-le - lu - jah, hal - le - lu-jah!

PSALM 114 TONE VIIb

1 *When Is̈ - rael came oút of É-gypt,**
   the house of Jacob from a péo-ple of stránge speech,
2 Judah became God's sánc-tu-ár-y*
   and Israel hís do-mín-ion.

(continued)

REFRAIN

BCP, p. 756

REFRAIN ALLELUIA VII

Hal-le-lu-jah, hal-le-lu-jah, hal-le-lu-jah!

PSALM 114 TONE VII*b*

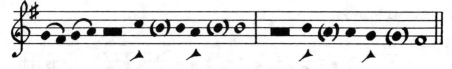

3 *The sea* be-héld it ánd fled;*
   Jordan túrned and wént back.
4 The móun-tains skípped like rams,*
   and the little hílls like yoúng sheep.

REFRAIN

5 *What ailed* you, O séa, that yóu fled?*
   O Jordan, thát you túrned back?
6 You mountains, thát you skípped like rams?*
   you little hílls like yoúng sheep?

REFRAIN

7 *Trem-ble*, O earth, at the prés-ence óf the Lord,*
   at the presence of the Gód of Já-cob,
8 Who turned the hard rock into a poól of wá-ter*
   and flint-stone in-tó a flów-ing spring.

REFRAIN

IF PREFERRED, THE PSALM MAY

BE SUNG WITHOUT THE REFRAIN

(SEE THE FOLLOWING PAGE)

PSALM 114   TONE VII*b*

1 *Hăl - lĕ -* lujah!
   When Israel came oút of É-gypt,*
      the house of Jacob from a péo-ple of stránge speech,

2 Judah became God's sánc-tu-ár-y*
      and Israel hís do-mín-ion.

3 The sea be-héld it ánd fled;*
      Jordan túrned and wént back.

4 The móun-tains skípped like rams,*
      and the little hílls like yoúng sheep.

5 What ailed you, O séa, that yóu fled?*
      O Jordan, thát you túrned back?

6 You mountains, thát you skípped like rams?*
      you little hílls like yoúng sheep?

7 Tremble, O earth, at the prés-ence óf the Lord,*
      at the presence of the Gód of Já-cob,

8 Who turned the hard rock into a poól of wá-ter*
      and flint-stone in-tó a flów-ing spring.

Easter Day A - *Principal Service (morning)*

REFRAIN

On this day the Lord has act-ed;

we will re-joice and be glad in it.

PSALM 118   TONE VIIIg

14 *The LORD* is my strength and my song,*
    and he has become / my sal-va-tion.
15 There is a sound of exultation and vic-to-ry*
    in the tents / of the right-eous.

REFRAIN

16 *"The right* hand of the LORD has tri-umphed!*
    the right hand of the LORD is exalted!
    the right hand of the / LORD has tri-umphed!"
17 I shall not die, but live,*
    and declare the / works of the LORD.

REFRAIN

22 *The same* stone which the builders re-ject-ed*
    has become / the chief cor-ner-stone.
23 This is the LORD's do-ing,*
    and it is mar - / vel-ous in our eyes.

REFRAIN

ALLELUIA VIII

Al - le - lu - ia, al-le-lu - ia, al - le-lu-ia.

VERSE (1 Cor. 5:7,8)   TONE VIII*g*

Christ our Passover is sacri-ficed for us:*

therefore let us keep the feast.

REFRAIN　　　　　　　　　　　　　　　ALLELUIA VII

Hal-le-lu-jah, hal-le-lu-jah, hal-le-lu-jah!

PSALM 114　　　　　　　　　　　　　　TONE VII*b*

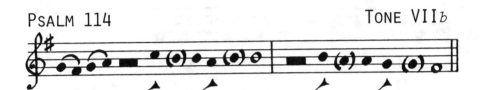

1　Hal-le-lujah!
　　When Israel came oút of É-gypt,*
　　　the house of Jacob from a péo-ple of stránge speech,
2　Judah became God's sánc-tu-ár-y*
　　and Israel hís do-mín-ion.

　　　　　　　　　　　　　　　　　　　REFRAIN

3　The sea be-héld it ánd fled;*
　　Jordan túrned and wént back.
4　The móun-tains skípped like rams,*
　　and the little hílls like yoúng sheep.

　　　　　　　　　　　　　　　　　　　REFRAIN

5　What ailed you, O séa, that yóu fled?*
　　O Jordan, thát you túrned back?
6　You mountains, thát you skípped like rams?*
　　you little hílls like yoúng sheep?

　　　　　　　　　　　　　　　　　　　REFRAIN

7　Trem-ble, O earth, at the prés-ence óf the Lord,*
　　at the presence of the Gód of Já-cob,
8　Who turned the hard rock into a poól of wá-ter*
　　and flint-stone in-tó a flów-ing spring.

　　　　　　　　　　　　　　　　　　　REFRAIN

ALLELUIA AS AT PRINCIPAL SERVICE
　　　(MORNING)

　　　　　　　　　　　　　　　　BCP, p. 756

REFRAIN

On this day the Lord has act-ed;

we will re-joice and be glad in it.

PSALM 118   TONE VIII*g*

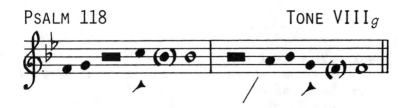

14 *The LORD* is my strength and my sóng,*
       and he has become / my sal-vá-tion.
15 There is a sound of exultation and víc-to-ry*
       in the tents / of the ríght-eous.
                                        REFRAIN

16 *"The right* hand of the LORD has trí-umphed!*
       the right hand of the LORD is exalted!
       the right hand of the / LORD has trí-umphed!"
17 I shall not die, but líve,*
       and declare the / works of thé LORD.
                                        REFRAIN

22 *The same* stone which the builders re-jéct-ed*
       has become / the chief cór-ner-stone.
23 This is the LORD'S dó-ing,*
       and it is mar - / vel-ous ín our eyes.
                                        REFRAIN

        ALLELUIA AS AT PRINCIPAL SERVICE
                   (MORNING)

Easter Day ABC - *Evening Service*

Refrain

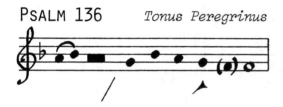

For his mer-cy en-dures for ev - er.

Psalm 136   *Tonus Peregrinus*

1 *Gíve* thanks to / the LORD, for hé is good,*

> REFRAIN

2 *Gíve* thanks / to the God óf gods,*

> REFRAIN

3 *Gíve* thanks / to the Lord óf lords,*

> REFRAIN

10 *Who* struck down the / first-born of É-gypt,*

> REFRAIN

11 *And* brought out Isra - / el from a-móng them,*

> REFRAIN

12 *With* a mighty / hand and a strétched-out arm,*

> REFRAIN

13 *Who* divided / the Red Sea ín two,*

> REFRAIN

14 *And* made Israel to / pass through the mídst of it,*

> REFRAIN

15 *But* swept Pharaoh and his army / in-to the Réd Sea,*

> REFRAIN

(continued)

BCP, p. 789

REFRAIN

For his mer-cy en-dures for ev - er.

PSALM 136 *Tonus Peregrinus*

16 *Who* led his peo - / ple through the wíl-der-ness,*

REFRAIN

23 *Who* remembered / us in our lów es-tate,*

REFRAIN

24 *And* delivered / us from our én-e-mies,*

REFRAIN

25 *Who* gives / food to all créa-tures,*

REFRAIN

26 *Give* thanks to / the God of héav-en,*

REFRAIN

REFRAIN   ALLELUIA VIII

Hal-le - lu - jah, hal-le-lu - jah, hal - le-lu-jah!

PSALM 16   TONE VIII*g*

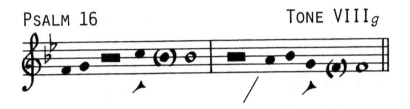

8 *I have* set the LORD always be-fóre me;*
    because he is at my right / hand I sháll not fall.

                          REFRAIN

9 *My heart*, therefore, is glad, and my spirit
                 re-joíc-es;*
    my body al - / so shall rést in hope.

                          REFRAIN

10 *For you* will not abandon me to the gráve,*
     nor let your ho - / ly one sée the Pit.

                          REFRAIN

11 *You will* show me the páth of life;*
     in your presence there is fullness of joy,
     and in your right hand are pleas - / ures for
           év-er-more.

                          REFRAIN

IN PLACE OF THE PSALM,
AN ALLELUIA VERSE MAY BE USED.
(SEE NEXT PAGE)

ALLELUIA VIII

Al-le - lu - ia, al-le-lu - ia, al - le-lu-ia.

VERSE (Psalm 118:24)

On this day the Lord has act-ed;*

we will re-joice and be glad in it.

MONDAY IN EASTER WEEK ABC

REFRAIN

Give thanks to the Lord, for he is good;

his mer-cy en-dures for ev-er.

ALTERNATE REFRAIN ALLELUIA VIII

Hal-le-lu-jah, hal-le-lu-jah, hal-le-lu-jah!

PSALM 118 TONE VIIIg

19 *O-pen* for me the gates of ríght-eous-ness;*
   I will enter them;
   I will offer / thanks to thé LORD.
20 "This is the gate of the LÓRD;*
   he who is right - / eous may én-ter."

REFRAIN

21 *I will* give thanks to you, for you án-swered me*
   and have become / my sal-vá-tion.
22 The same stone which the builders re-jéct-ed*
   has become / the chief cór-ner-stone.

REFRAIN

(continued)

REFRAIN

Give thanks to the Lord, for he is good;

his mer-cy en-dures for ev-er.

ALTERNATE REFRAIN   ALLELUIA VIII

Hal-le - lu - jah, hal-le-lu - jah, hal - le-lu-jah!

PSALM 118   TONE VIIIg

23 *This is* the LORD'S dó-ing,*
    and it is mar - / vel-ous ín our eyes.
24 On this day the LORD has áct-ed;*
    we will rejoice / and be glád in it.

REFRAIN

IN PLACE OF THE PSALM,
AN ALLELUIA VERSE MAY BE USED.
(SEE NEXT PAGE)

Monday in Easter Week ABC - *Alleluia Verse Alternate*

Alleluia VIII

Al-le - lu - ia, al-le-lu - ia, al - le-lu-ia.

Verse   (Psalm 118:24)

On this day the Lord has act-ed;*

we will re-joice and be glad in it.

REFRAIN   **ALLELUIA VI**

Hal-le-lu-jah, hal - le-lu-jah, hal-le - lu - jah!

PSALM 33   **TONE VI**

1 *Re - joíce* in the LORD, / you ríght-eous;*
   it is good for the just / to síng práis-es.
2 Praise the LORD / with thé harp;*
   play to him upon the psal - / te-rÿ añd lyre.

REFRAIN

18 *Be - holᵈ*, the eye of the LORD is upon those / who
                    féar him,*
   on those who / wait üp-ón his love,
19 To pluck / their líves from death,*
   and to feed them in / time öf fám-ine.

REFRAIN

20 *Our soül* waits / for thé LORD;*
   he is our / help añd oúr shield.
21 Indeed, our heart rejoic - / es ín him,*
   for in his holy / Name wë pút our trust.

REFRAIN

IN PLACE OF THE PSALM,
AN ALLELUIA VERSE MAY BE USED,
OR PSALM 118 AS ON MONDAY.

ALLELUIA AS ON MONDAY

Wednesday in Easter Week ABC

REFRAIN   ALLELUIA VII

Hal-le-lu-jah, hal-le-lu-jah, hal-le-lu-jah!

PSALM 105   TONE VIIb

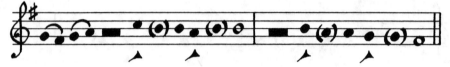

1 *Give thanks* to the LORD and cáll up-ón his Name;*
   make known his deeds a-móng the péo-ples.
2 Sing to him, sing práis-es tó him,*
   and speak of áll his már-velous works.

                                           REFRAIN

3 *Glo-ry* —— ín his hó-ly Name;*
   let the hearts of those who seék the LÓRD re-joice.
4 Search for the LÓRD and hís strength;*
   con-tín-ual-ly seék his face.

                                           REFRAIN

5 *Re-mem*-ber the már-vels hé has done,*
   his wonders and the júdg-ments óf his mouth,
6 O offspring of A-bra-hám his sér-vant,*
   O children of Já-cob his chó-sen.

                                           REFRAIN

7 —— He ís the LÓRD our God;*
   his judgments pre-váil in áll the world.
8 He has always been mindful óf his cóv-e-nant,*
   the promise he made for a thousand gén-er-á-tions.

                                           REFRAIN

IN PLACE OF THE PSALM,
AN ALLELUIA VERSE MAY BE USED,
OR PSALM 118 AS ON MONDAY.

ALLELUIA AS ON MONDAY

REFRAIN   ALLELUIA VII

Hal-le-lu-jah, hal-le-lu-jah, hal-le-lu-jah!

PSALM 8   TONE VIIb

1 — O LÓRD our Góv-er-nor,*
     how exalted is your Náme in áll the world!
2 Out of the mouths of ín-fants and chíl-dren*
     your majesty is praised a-bóve the héav-ens.

                                    REFRAIN

4 *When I* consider your heavens, the wórk of your fín-gers,*
     the moon and the stars you have sét in their cóur-ses,
5 What is man that you should be mínd-ful óf him?*
     the son of man that yóu should séek him out?

                                    REFRAIN

6 *You have* made him but little lower thán the án-gels;*
     you adorn him with gló-ry and hón-or;
7 You give him mastery over the wórks of yóur hands;*
     you put all things ún-der hís feet.

                                    REFRAIN

            IN PLACE OF THE PSALM,
       AN ALLELUIA VERSE MAY BE USED,
       OR PSALM 118 AS ON MONDAY.

          ALLELUIA AS ON MONDAY

                                    BCP, p. 592

THURSDAY IN EASTER WEEK ABC

REFRAIN   ALLELUIA VII

Hal-le-lu - jah, hal - le - lu - jah, hal - le - lu-jah!

PSALM 114   TONE VII*b*

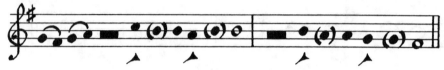

1 *When Is* - rael came oút of É-gypt,*
    the house of Jacob from a péo-ple of stránge speech,
2 Judah became God's sánc-tu-ár-y*
    and Israel hís do-mín-ion.

                              REFRAIN

3 *The sea* be-héld it añd fled;*
    Jordan túrned and wént back.
4 The móun-tains skípped like rams,*
    and the little hílls like yoúng sheep.

                              REFRAIN

5 *What ailed* you, O séa, that yóu fled?*
    O Jordan, thát you túrned back?
6 You mountains, thát you skípped like rams?*
    you little hílls like yoúng sheep?

                              REFRAIN

7 *Trem - ble*, O earth, at the prés-ence óf the Lord,*
    at the presence of the Gód of Já-cob,
8 Who turned the hard rock into a poól of wá-ter*
    and flint-stone in-tó a flów-ing spring.

                              REFRAIN

IN PLACE OF THE PSALM,
AN ALLELUIA VERSE MAY BE USED,
OR PSALM 118 AS ON MONDAY.

ALLELUIA AS ON MONDAY

REFRAIN   ALLELUIA VIII

Hal-le - lu - jah, hal-le-lu - jah, hal - le-lu-jah!

PSALM 116   TONE VIIIg

1 *I love* the LORD, because he has heard the voice of
        my sup-pli-cá-tion,*
   because he has inclined his ear to me whenever
        I / called up-ón him.

                              REFRAIN

2 *The cords* of death entangled me;
   the grip of the grave took hóld of me;*
     I came to / grief and sór-row.
3 Then I called upon the Name of the LÓRD:*
   "O LORD, I / pray you, sáve my life."

                              REFRAIN

5 *The LORD* watches over the ín-no-cent;*
   I was brought very low, / and he hélped me.
6 Turn again to your rest, Ó my soul,*
   for the LORD has / treat-ed yóu well.

                              REFRAIN

7 *For you* have rescued my lífe from death,*
   my eyes from tears, and my / feet from stúm-bling.
8 I will walk in the presence of the LÓRD*
   in the land / of the lív-ing.

                              REFRAIN

IN PLACE OF THE PSALM,
AN ALLELUIA VERSE MAY BE USED,
OR PSALM 118 AS ON MONDAY.

ALLELUIA AS ON MONDAY

BCP, p. 759

REFRAIN   ALLELUIA VIII

Hal-le - lu - jah, hal-le-lu - jah, hal - le-lu-jah!

PSALM 118   TONE VIII*g*

1 *Give thanks* to the LORD, for hé is good;*
      his mercy en - / dures for év-er.
14 The LORD is my strength and my sóng,*
      and he has become / my sal-vá-tion.

                                           REFRAIN

15 *There is* a sound of exultation and víc-to-ry*
      in the tents / of the ríght-eous:
16 "The right hand of the LORD has trí-umphed!*
      the right hand of the LORD is exalted!
      the right hand of the / LORD has trí-umphed!"

                                           REFRAIN

17 *I shall* not die, but líve,*
      and declare the / works of thé LORD.
18 The LORD has punished me sóre-ly,*
      but he did not hand me / o-ver tó death.

                                           REFRAIN

                 IN PLACE OF THE PSALM,
         AN ALLELUIA VERSE MAY BE USED,
            OR PSALM 118 AS ON MONDAY.

            ALLELUIA AS ON MONDAY

                                           BCP, p. 760

REFRAIN

Give thanks to the Lord, for he is good;

his mer-cy en-dures for ev-er.

ALTERNATE REFRAIN   ALLELUIA VIII

Hal-le -lu -jah, hal-le-lu -jah, hal -le-lu-jah!

PSALM 118   TONE VIII*g*

19 *O - pen* for me the gates of right-eous-ness;*
        I will enter them;
        I will offer / thanks to the LORD.
20 "This is the gate of the LORD;*
        he who is right - / eous may én-ter."

                                    REFRAIN

21 *I will* give thanks to you, for you án-swered me*
        and have become / my sal-vá-tion.
22 The same stone which the builders re-jéct-ed*
        has become / the chief cór-ner-stone.

                                    REFRAIN

(continued)   BCP, p. 762

REFRAIN

Give thanks to the Lord, for he is good;

his mer-cy en-dures for ev-er.

ALTERNATE REFRAIN   **ALLELUIA VIII**

Hal-le -lu -jah, hal-le-lu -jah, hal -le-lu-jah!

PSALM 118   **TONE VIII***g*

23 *This is* the LORD'S dó-ing,*
      and it is mar - / vel-ous iń our eyes.
24 On this day the LORD has áct-ed;*
      we will rejoice / and be glád in it.

                                        REFRAIN

Alleluia VIII

Al-le -lu -ia, al-le-lu -ia, al -le-lu-ia.

Verse (John 20:29)   Tone VIII*g*

You be - lieve in me, Thomas, because you have seen me;*

blessed are those who have not seen and yet be-lieve.

REFRAIN   ALLELUIA IV

Hal-le-lu-jah, hal-le -lu -jah, hal-le -lu-jah!

PSALM 111   TONE IVe

1 *Hal - lĕ - lujah!*
   I will give thanks to the LORD / with my whóle heart,*
      in the assembly of the upright, in / the
                        con-gr̆e-g̈ä-tion.
2 Great are the deeds / of the LORD!*
      they are studied by / all who dë-light iñ them.

                                    REFRAIN

3 *His work* is full of majes - / ty and splen-dor,*
      and his righteousness / en-dures för év̈-er.
4 He makes his marvelous works to / be re-mém-bered;*
      the LORD is gracious and / full of cöm-p̈äs-sion.

                                    REFRAIN

9 *He sent* redemption to his people;
   he commanded his cove - / nant for év̈-er;*
      holy and / awe-some is̈ hís Name.
10 The fear of the LORD is the begin - / ning of ẃis-dom;*
      those who act accordingly have a good understanding;
      his praise / en-dures för év̈-er.

                                    REFRAIN

BCP, p. 754

ALLELUIA VII

Al-le-lu -ia, al -le -lu -ia, al -le - lu-ia.

VERSE   (John 20:29)   TONE VIIb

You be - lieve in me, Thomas, be-cause you have

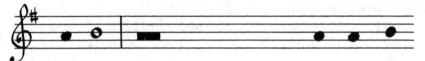

seen me;* blessed are those who have not seen

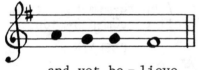

and yet be - lieve.

3 Easter A

REFRAIN

I will walk in the pres-ence of the Lord

in the land of the liv - ing.

ALTERNATE REFRAIN　　　　　　**ALLELUIA III**

Hal-le -lu - jah, hal-le -lu-jah, hal-le -lu-jah!

PSALM 116　　　　　　**TONE IIIb**

10　*How shäll* —— Í re-páy thë LORD*
　　for all the good things he / has dóne for me?
11　I will lift up the cúp of sal-vä-tion*
　　and call upon the Name / of thé LORD.

　　　　　　　　　　　　　　　　REFRAIN

12　*I wïll* fulfill my vóws to thë LORD*
　　in the presence of all / his péo-ple.
13　Precious in the sight of thë LORD*
　　is the death of / his sér-vants.

　　　　　　　　　　　　　　　　REFRAIN

(continued)　　　　　　　　　　*BCP, p. 759*

REFRAIN

I will walk in the pres-ence of the Lord

in the land of the liv-ing.

ALTERNATE REFRAIN   ALLELUIA III

Hal-le-lu - jah, hal-le-lu-jah, hal-le-lu-jah!

PSALM 116   TONE IIIb

14 *O LORD,* —— Í am your sẽr-vant;*
     I am your servant and the child of your handmaid;
     you have freed / me fróm my bonds.
15 I will offer you the sacrifice óf thanks-gĩv-ing*
     and call upon the Name / of thé LORD.

                                  REFRAIN

16 *I will* fulfill my vóws to thẽ LORD*
     in the presence of all / his péo-ple,
17 In the coúrts of the LÓRD'S house,*
     in the midst of you, O Jerusalem.
     Hal - / le-lú-jah!

                                    REFRAIN

BCP, p. 759

ALLELUIA I

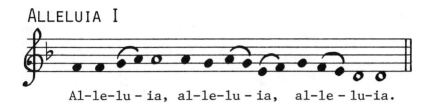

Al-le-lu - ia, al-le-lu - ia, al-le - lu-ia.

VERSE   (Luke 24:32)   TONE I*f*

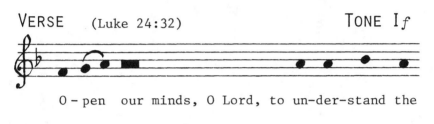

O - pen   our minds, O Lord, to un-der-stand the

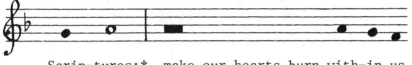

Scrip-tures;* make our hearts burn with-in us

when you speak.

4 Easter A

REFRAIN

The Lord is my shep-herd; I shall not be in want.

ALTERNATE REFRAIN **ALLELUIA IV**

Hal-le-lu-jah, hal-le -lu -jah, hal-le -lu-jah!

PSALM 23 **TONE IV*e***

2 *He makes* me lie down / in green pás-tures*
   and leads me / be-side still wä-ters.
3 He re - / vives my sóul*
   and guides me along right / path-ways för
          hís Name's sake.

                    REFRAIN

4a *Though I* walk through the valley of the sha - / dow
          of déath,
   —— / I shall feär nó ë-vil;
4b For / you are with me;*
   your rod and / your staff, thëy cóm-fort me.

                    REFRAIN

5 *You spread* a table before me in the presence
          of / those who tróub-le me;*
   you have anointed my head with oil,
   and my / cup is rün-níing ö-ver.
6 Surely your goodness and mercy shall follow me
          all the days / of my lífe,*
   and I will dwell in the house of / the LORD för év-er.

                    REFRAIN

BCP, p. 612

ALLELUIA IV

Al-le-lu-ia, al-le -lu -ia, al-le -lu-ia.

VERSE (John 10:14)   TONE IV*e*

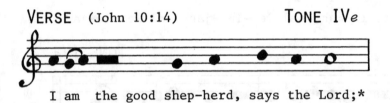

I am the good shep-herd, says the Lord;*

I know my sheep, and my sheep know me.

5 Easter A

REFRAIN

Be joy-ful in God, all you lands.

ALTERNATE REFRAIN   **ALLELUIA V**

Hal-le-lu-jah, hal-le-lu -jah, hal -le -lu-jah!

PSALM 66   **TONE V***a*

1 *Be joy* - ful in God, all you lánds;*
    sing the glory of his Name;
    sing the gló-ry óf his praise.
2 Say to God, "How awesome are your déeds!*
    because of your great strength your enemies
                         críñge be-fóre you.

                               REFRAIN

3 *All the* earth bows down be-fóre you,*
    sings to you, siñgs out yóur Name."
4 Come now and see the wórks of God,*
    how wonderful he is in his doing towa̧rd all péo-ple.

                               REFRAIN

5 *He turned* the sea into dry land,
    so that they went through the water on fóot,*
    and thére we re-jóiced in him.
6 In his might he rules for ever;
    his eyes keep watch over the ná-tions;*
    let no rebel rise úp a-gáinst him.

                               REFRAIN

(continued)   BCP, p. 673

5 Easter A   *(continuation)*

Refrain

Be joy-ful in God, all you lands.

Alternate Refrain   **Alleluia V**

Hal-le-lu-jah, hal-le-lu -jah, hal -le -lu-jah!

Psalm 66   **Tone V**α

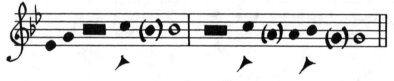

7 *Bless our* God, you péo-ples;*
    make the voice of his práise to bé heard;
8 Who holds our soúls in life,*
    and will not al-lów our feét to slip.

                                    REFRAIN

BCP, p. 673

5 EASTER A

ALLELUIA I

Al-le-lu - ia, al-le-lu - ia, al-le - lu-ia.

VERSE (John 14:6)   TONE I*f*

I am   the way, the truth, and the life;*

no one comes to the Fa-ther, but by   me.

Refrain

Sing to the Lord a new song.

Alternate Refrain   Alleluia VI

Hal-le-lu-jah, hal -le-lu-jah,   hal-le -lu -jah!

Psalm 148   Tone VI

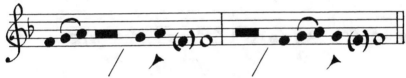

7 *Praise the̅* LORD from / the eárth,*
  you sea - / mon-stërs áńd all deeps;
8 Fire and hail, snow / and fóg,
  tempestuous wind, / do-iñg hís will;

REFRAIN

9 *Moun - tains̅* and / all hílls,*
  fruit trees / and äll cé-dars;
10 Wild beasts and / all cát-tle,*
  creeping / things añd wiñged birds;

REFRAIN

11 *Kings öf* the earth and / all péo-ples,*
  princes and / rul-eïs óf the world;
12 Young men / and máid-ens,*
  old and / young tö-géth-er.

REFRAIN

(continued)   *BCP, p. 806*

REFRAIN

Sing to the Lord a new song.

ALTERNATE REFRAIN   ALLELUIA VI

Hal-le-lu-jah, hal-le-lu-jah, hal-le-lu-jah!

PSALM 148   TONE VI

13 *Let them* praise the Name of / the LÓRD,*
     for his Name only is exalted,
     his splendor is over / earth aïd heáv-en.
14 He has raised up strength for his people
     and praise for all his loy- / al sér-vants,*
      the children of Israel, a people who are near him,
     / Hal-lë-lú-jah!

                       REFRAIN

BCP, p. 806

Alleluia VII

Al-le-lu -ia, al -le -lu -ia, al -le - lu-ia.

Verse   (John 15:4,5)   Tone VIIb

A - bide in me as I in you, says the Lord;*

I am the vine and you are the branch-es.

Ascension Day A

Refrain

I am with you al-ways, to the close of the age.

Alternate Refrain   Alleluia VIII

Hal-le -lu -jah, hal-le-lu -jah, hal -le-lu-jah!

Psalm 110   Tone VIIIc

1 *The LORD* said to my Lord, "Sit at my ríght hand,*
      until I make your ene - / mies your fóot-stool."

                                        REFRAIN

2 *The LORD* will send the scepter of your power out
                        of Zí-on,*
      saying, "Rule over your enemies / round a-bóut you.

                                        REFRAIN

3 *Prince - ly* state has been yours from the day of
                    your bírth;*
      in the beauty of holiness have I begotten you,
      like dew from the womb / of the mórn-ing."

                                        REFRAIN

4 *The LORD* has sworn and he will nót re-cant:*
      "You are a priest for ever after the
                        order / of Mel-chi-ze-dek."

                                        REFRAIN

REFRAIN

God has gone up with a   shout, the Lord with

the sound   of the   ram's-horn.

ALTERNATE REFRAIN   ALLELUIA VII

Hal-le-lu -jah, hal -le -lu -jah, hal -le - lu-jah!

PSALM 47   TONE VIIb

1 *Cl̈ap yoür* hands, áll you péo-ples;*
     shout to God ẃith a crý of joy.
2 For the LORD Most High is tó be feared;*
     he is the great Kíng o-ver áll the earth.

                                   REFRAIN

5 *G̈öd häs* gone úp with á shout,*
     the LORD with the soúnd of the rám's-horn.
6 Sing praises to Gód, sing práis-es;*
     sing praises to our Kíng, sing práis-es.

                                   REFRAIN

(continued)   BCP, p. 650

REFRAIN

God has gone up with a   shout, the Lord with

the sound   of the   ram's-horn.

ALTERNATE REFRAIN   ALLELUIA VII

Hal-le-lu -jah, hal -le -lu -jah, hal -le - lu-jah!

PSALM 47   TONE VII*b*

7 *För Göd* is Kińg of áll the earth;*
    sing práis-es with áll your skill.
8 God reigns ó-ver the ńa-tions;*
    God sits up-óń his hó-ly throne.

REFRAIN

ALLELUIA IV

Al-le-lu-ia, al-le -lu -ia, al-le -lu-ia.

VERSE (Matt. 28:19-20)   TONE IVe

Go and make disciples of all na-tions;*

I am with you always, to the close of the age.

7 Easter A

REFRAIN

God has gone up with a shout, the Lord with

the sound of the ram's-horn.

ALTERNATE REFRAIN   ALLELUIA VII

Hal-le-lu -jah, hal -le -lu -jah, hal -le - lu-jah!

PSALM 47   TONE VII*b*

1 *Clặp yoür* hands, áll you péo-ples;*
       shout to God w̓ith a cŕy of joy.
2 For the LORD Most High is tó be feared;*
       he is the great Kiṅg o-ver áll the earth.

REFRAIN

5 *Göd häs* gone úp with á shout,*
       the LORD with the soúnd of the rám's-horn.
6 Sing praises to Gód, sing práis-es;*
       sing praises to our Kiṅg, sing práis-es.

REFRAIN

(continued)   *BCP, p. 650*

7 EASTER A   *(continuation)*

REFRAIN

God has gone up with a   shout, the Lord with

the sound   of the   ram's-horn.

ALTERNATE REFRAIN   **ALLELUIA VII**

Hal-le-lu -jah, hal -le -lu -jah, hal -le - lu-jah!

PSALM 47   **TONE VIIb**

7 *För Göd* is Kińg of áll the earth;*
     sing práis-es with áll your skill.
8 God reigns ó-ver the ńa-tions;*
     God sits up-oń his hó-ly throne.

REFRAIN

REFRAIN

Sing to God, O king-doms of the earth;

sing prais-es to the Lord.

ALTERNATE REFRAIN　　　ALLELUIA VII

Hal-le-lu-jah, hal-le-lu-jah, hal-le-lu-jah!

PSALM 68　　　　　　　TONE VIIb

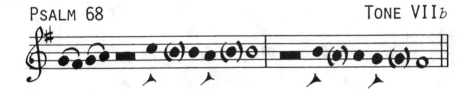

4　*Sing to* God, sing praises to his Name;
　　exalt him who rides up-on the heav-ens;*
　　　YAHWEH is his Name, re-joice be-fore him!
5　Father of orphans, de-fend-er of wid-ows,*
　　God in his holy hab-i-ta-tion!

REFRAIN

7　*O God,* when you went forth be-fore your peo-ple,*
　　when you marched through the wil-der-ness,
8　The earth shook, and the skies poured down rain,
　　at the presence of God, the God of Si-nai,*
　　at the presence of God, the God of Is-ra-el.

REFRAIN

(continued)　　　　　　　　　*BCP, p. 676*

REFRAIN

Sing to God, O king-doms of the earth;

sing prais - es to the Lord.

ALTERNATE REFRAIN   ALLELUIA VII

Hal-le-lu -jah, hal -le -lu -jah, hal -le - lu-jah!

PSALM 68   TONE VII*b*

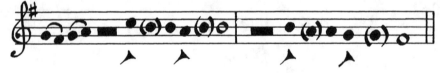

17 *The chär* - iots of God are twenty thousand,
    even thóu-sands of thóu-sands;*
      the Lord comes in holi-néss from Sí-nai.
18 You have gone up on high and led captivity captive;
    you have received gifts even fróm your én-e-mies,*
      that the LORD God might dwéll a-móng them.

                            REFRAIN

ALLELUIA I

Al-le-lu - ia, al-le-lu - ia, al-le - lu-ia.

VERSE   (John 14:18)   TONE I*f*

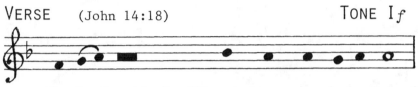

The Lord said, I will not leave you des-o-late;*

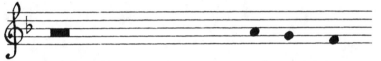

I will come back to you, and your hearts

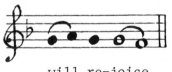

will re-joice.

Vigil of Pentecost ABC *(or Early Service)*

REFRAIN

Hap-py is the na-tion whose God is the Lord.

PSALM 33   **TONE VI**

13 *The LORD* looks down / from héav-en,*
      and beholds all the / peo-plë ín the world.
14 From where he sits enthroned / he túrns his gaze*
      on all / who dwëll ón the earth.
15 He fashions all / the heárts of them*
      and un - / der-ständs áll their works.

                                   REFRAIN

16 *There is* no king that can be saved by a might - / y
                  ár-my;*
      a strong man is not delivered / by hïs gréat strength.
18 Behold, the eye of the LORD is upon those / who
                  féar him,*
      on those who wait / up-ön hís love,
19 To pluck / their líves from death,*
      and to feed them in / time öf fám-ine.

                                   REFRAIN

20 *Our soül* waits / for thé LORD;*
      he is our / help aňd oúr shield.
21 Indeed, our heart rejoic - / es ín him,*
      for in his holy / Name wë pút our trust.
22 Let your loving-kindness, O LORD, be / up-ón us,*
      as we have / put oür trúst in you.

                                   REFRAIN

Vigil of Pentecost ABC *(or Early Service)*

REFRAIN

He has made us a king-dom of priests

and a ho-ly na-tion.

CANTICLE 13   TONE VIIIg

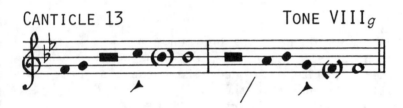

1 *Glo - ry* to you, Lord God of our fá-thers;*
     you are worthy of praise; / glo-ry tó you.
2 Glory to you for the radiance of your hó-ly Name;*
     we will praise you and highly exalt / you for év-er.

                              REFRAIN

3 *Glo - ry* to you in the splendor of your tém-ple;*
     on the throne of your majesty, / glo-ry tó you.
4 Glory to you, seated between the Chér-u-bim;*
     we will praise you and highly exalt / you for év-er.

                              REFRAIN

5 *Glo - ry* to you, beholding the dépths;*
     in the high vault of heaven, / glo-ry tó you.
6 Glory to you, Father, Son, and Holy Spír-it;*
     we will praise you and highly exalt / you for év-er.

                              REFRAIN

BCP, p. 90

VIGIL OF PENTECOST ABC *(or Early Service)*

REFRAIN

With the Lord there is mer-cy; with him there

is plen-te-ous re - demp - tion.

PSALM 130   TONE IIIb

1 *Out of* the depths have I called to you, O LORD;
   LÓRD, hear mÿ voice;*
      let your ears consider well the voice of
                  my sup - / pli-cá-tion.

                                    REFRAIN

2 *If yöu*, LORD, were to note whát is dóne ä-miss,*
   O Lord, / who cóuld stand?
3 For there is for-gíve-ness wïth you;*
   therefore / you sháll be feared.

                                    REFRAIN

4 *I wait* for the LORD; my sóul waits fór him;*
   in his word / is mÿ hope.
5 My soul waits for the LORD,
   more than watchmen fór the mórn-ing,*
      more than watchmen for / the mórn-ing.

                                    REFRAIN

6 *O Is* - rael, wáit for thë LORD,*
   for with the LORD there / is mér-cy;*
7 With him there is plente-oús re-démp-tion,*
   and he shall redeem Israel / from áll their sins.

                                    REFRAIN
                                    BCP, p. 784

Vigil of Pentecost ABC *(or Early Service)*

REFRAIN

You shall draw wa-ter with re - joic-ing

from the springs of sal-va - tion.

CANTICLE 9   TONE VIIIg

1 *Sure - ly*, it is God who sáves me;*
    I will trust in him and / not be á-fraid.
2 For the Lord is my stronghold and my súre de-fense,*
    and he will / be my Sáv-ior.

                                    REFRAIN

4 *And on* that day you shall sáy,*
    Give thanks to the Lord and / call up-ón his Name;
5 Make his deeds known among the péo-ples;*
    see that they remember that his Name / is ex-ált-ed.

                                    REFRAIN

6 *Sing the* praises of the Lord, for he has done
                        gréat things,*
    and this is / known in áll the world.
7 Cry aloud, inhabitants of Zion, ring out your jóy,*
    for the great one in the midst of you is
                        the Holy / One of Iś-ra-el.

                                    REFRAIN

Vigil of Pentecost ABC *(or Early Service)*

Refrain

Send forth your Spir-it, O Lord,

and re - new the face of the earth.

Alternate Refrain   Alleluia VIII

Hal-le - lu - jah, hal-le-lu - jah, hal - le-lu-jah!

Psalm 104   Tone VIII*g*

25 *O LORD,* how manifold are your wórks!*
    in wisdom you have made them all;
    the earth is full / of your créa-tures.
26 Yonder is the great and wide sea
    with its living things too many to núm-ber,*
    crea - / tures both smáll and great.

                    REFRAIN

28 *All of* them loók to you*
    to give them their food / in due séa-son.
29 You give it to them; they gáth-er it;*
    you open your hand, and they are / filled with
            good things.

                    REFRAIN

(continued)

BCP, p. 730

REFRAIN

Send forth your Spir-it, O Lord,

and re - new the face of the earth.

ALTERNATE REFRAIN   ALLELUIA VIII

Hal-le - lu - jah, hal-le-lu - jah, hal - le-lu-jah!

PSALM 104   TONE VIII*g*

30 *You hide* your face, and they are tér-ri-fied;*
    you take away their breath,
    and they die and re - / turn to théir dust.
31 You send forth your Spirit, and they are cre-á-ted;*
    and so you renew the / face of thé earth.

                       REFRAIN

32 *May the* glory of the LORD endure for év-er;*
    may the LORD re - / joice in áll his works.
35 May these words of mine pleáse him;*
    I will re - / joice in thé LORD.

                       REFRAIN

BCP, p. 736

Vigil of Pentecost ABC *(or Early Service)*

Alleluia II

Al – le-lu-ia, al-le-lu-ia, al-le-lu-ia.

Verse   Tone II

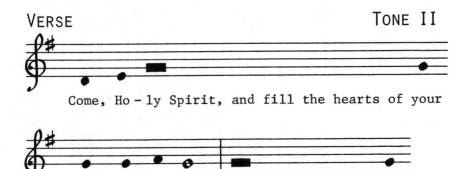

Come, Ho – ly Spirit, and fill the hearts of your

faith-ful peo-ple,* and kindle in them the

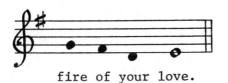

fire of your love.

REFRAIN

Send forth your Spir-it, O Lord,

and re - new the face of the earth.

ALTERNATE REFRAIN   ALLELUIA VIII

Hal-le - lu - jah, hal-le-lu - jah, hal - le-lu-jah!

PSALM 104   TONE VIIIg

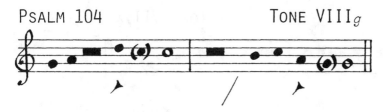

25   *O LORD*, how manifold are your wórks!*
         in wisdom you have made them all;
         the earth is full / of your créa-tures.
26   Yonder is the great and wide sea
         with its living things too many to núm-ber,*
         crea - / tures both smáll and great.

                                        REFRAIN

28   *All of* them loók to you*
         to give them their food / in due séa-son.
29   You give it to them; they gáth-er it;*
         you open your hand, and they are / filled with
                        goód things.

                                        REFRAIN

(continued)

                                        BCP, p. 736

REFRAIN

Send forth your Spir-it, O Lord,

and re - new the face of the earth.

ALTERNATE REFRAIN   ALLELUIA VIII

Hal-le - lu - jah, hal-le-lu - jah, hal - le-lu-jah!

PSALM 104   TONE VIII*g*

30 *You hide* your face, and they are tér-ri-fied;*
     you take away their breath,
     and they die and re - / turn to théir dust.
31 You send forth your Spirit, and they are cre-á-ted;*
     and so you renew the / face of thé earth.

                               REFRAIN

32 *May the* glory of the LORD endure for év-er;*
     may the LORD re - / joice in áll his works.
35 May these words of mine pleáse him;*
     I will re - / joice in thé LORD.

                               REFRAIN

REFRAIN

Hap-py is the na - tion whose God is the Lord.

PSALM 33   TONE V*a*

13 *The LORD* looks down from héav-en,*
    and beholds all the péo-ple ín the world.
14 From where he sits enthroned he túrns his gaze*
    on all who dwéll on thé earth.

                       REFRAIN

15 *He fash* - ions all the héarts of them*
    and un-der-stánds all théir works.
18 Behold, the eye of the LORD is upon those who
        féar him,*
    on those who wáit up-ón his love,

                       REFRAIN

19 *To pluck* their líves from death,*
    and to feed them in tíme of fám-ine.
20 Our soul waits for the LÓRD;*
    he is our hélp and oúr shield.

                       REFRAIN

21 *In* - *deed*, our heart rejoices in hím,*
    for in his holy Náme we pút our trust.
22 Let your loving-kindness, O LORD, be up-ón us,*
    as we have pút our trúst in you.

                       REFRAIN

ALLELUIA II

Al - le-lu-ia, al-le-lu-ia, al-le-lu-ia.

VERSE   TONE II

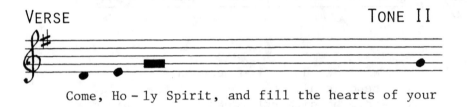

Come, Ho - ly Spirit, and fill the hearts of your

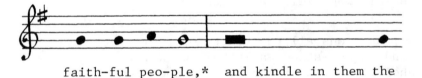

faith-ful peo-ple,*   and kindle in them the

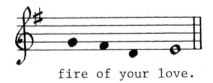

fire of your love.

TRINITY SUNDAY A

REFRAIN

Glo-ry to you, Fa-ther, Son, and Ho-ly Spir-it.

CANTICLE 2   TONE VIII*g*

1 *Bless - ed* art thou, O Lord God of our fá-thers;*
    praised and exalted above / all for év-er.
2 Blessed art thou for the Name of thy Má-jes-ty;*
    praised and exalted above / all for év-er.

REFRAIN

3 *Bless - ed* art thou in the temple of thy hó-li-ness;*
    praised and exalted above / all for év-er.
4 Blessed art thou that beholdest the depths,
    and dwellest between the Chér-u-bim;*
    praised and exalted above / all for év-er.
5 Blessed art thou on the glorious throne of thy
          king-dom;*
    praised and exalted above / all for év-er.

REFRAIN

6 *Bless - ed* art thou in the firmament of héav-en;*
    praised and exalted above / all for év-er.
7 Blessed art thou, O Father, Son, and Holy Spír-it;*
    praised and exalted above / all for év-er.

REFRAIN

Trinity Sunday A

Refrain

Glo-ry to you, Fa-ther, Son, and Ho-ly Spir-it.

Canticle 13   Tone VIII*g*

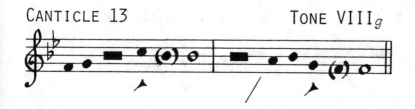

1 *Glo - ry* to you, Lord God of our fá-thers;*
     you are worthy of praise; / glo-ry tó you.
2 Glory to you for the radiance of your hó-ly Name;*
     we will praise you and highly exalt / you for év-er.

                                    REFRAIN

3 *Glo - ry* to you in the splendor of your tém-ple;*
     on the throne of your majesty, / glo-ry tó you.
4 Glory to you, seated between the Chér-u-bim;*
     we will praise you and highly exalt / you for év-er.

                                    REFRAIN

5 *Glo - ry* to you, beholding the depths;*
     in the high vault of heaven, / glo-ry tó you.
6 Glory to you, Father, Son, and Holy Spír-it;*
     we will praise you and highly exalt / you for év-er.

                                    REFRAIN

Trinity Sunday A

Refrain

Let eve-ry-thing that has breath praise the Lord.

Psalm 150   **Tone VIII*c***

1 *Hal - le -* lujah!
   Praise God in his holy tém-ple;*
      praise him in the firmament / of his pów-er.
2 Praise him for his mighty aćts;*
      praise him for his ex - / cel-lent gréat-ness.

                                        REFRAIN

3 *Praise him* with the blast of the rám's-horn;*
      praise him / with the lýre and harp.
4 Praise him with timbrel and dańce;*
      praise / him with stŕings and pipe.

                                        REFRAIN

5 *Praise him* with resounding cým-bals;*
      praise him with loud - / clang-ing cým-bals.
6 Let everything that has bréath*
      praise the LORD.
      / Hal-le-lú-jah!

                                        REFRAIN

BCP, p. 807

TRINITY SUNDAY A

ALLELUIA VIII

Al-le - lu - ia, al-le-lu - ia, al - le-lu-ia.

VERSE   (Rev. 1:4)   TONE VIIIg

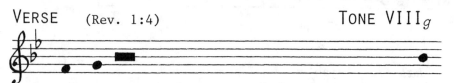

Glo - ry to the Father, and to the Son, and to the

Ho-ly Spir-it;* to God who is, and who was,

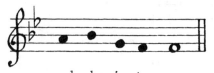

and who is to come.

PROPER 1 A

Same as 6 Epiphany A

PROPER 2 A

Same as 7 Epiphany A

PROPER 3 A

Same as 8 Epiphany A

PROPER 4 A

REFRAIN

In-to your hands I com-mend my spir - it.

PSALM 31   TONE I*g*

1 *In you,* O LORD, have I taken refuge;
   let me nёv-er be pút to shame;*
      deliver me / in your rĭght-eous-ness.
2 In-clĭne your eár to me;*
   make haste / to de-lĭv-er me.

REFRAIN

3 *Be my* strong rock, a castle to keep me safe,
   for your are my crág and my stróng-hold;*
      for the sake of your Name, lead / me and gŭide me.
4 Take me out of the net that they have sé-cret-ly
              sét for me,*
   for you / are my tŏwer of strength.

REFRAIN

5 *In - to* your hands I com-ménd my spír-it,*
   for you have redeemed me,
   O / LORD, O Gŏd of truth.
16 Make your face to shine up-on your sér-vant,*
   and in your loving - / kind-ness sǎve me.

REFRAIN

ALLELUIA - Ad libitum

BCP, p. 622

PROPER 5 A

REFRAIN

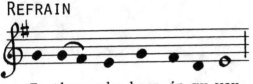

To those who keep in my way

will I show the sal-va - tion of God.

PSALM 50 TONE II

7 *Hear, O* my people, and I will speak:
   "O Israel, I will bear witness a-gáinst you;*
   for I am / God, yóur God.

8 I do not accuse you because of your sac-ri-fíc-es;*
   your offerings are always / be-fóre me.

   REFRAIN

9 *I will* take no bull-calf from your stálls,*
   nor he-goats out / of yóur pens;

10 For all the beasts of the forest are míne,*
   the herds in their thousands up - / on thé hills.

   REFRAIN

12 *If I* were hungry, I would not téll you,*
   for the whole world is mine and all that / is iñ it.

13 Do you think I eat the flesh of búlls,*
   or drink the / blood óf goats?

   REFRAIN

14 *Of - fer* to God a sacrifice of thanks-gív-ing*
   and make good your vows to / the Móst High.

15 Call upon me in the day of tróu-ble;*
   I will deliver you, and you / shall hón-or me.

   REFRAIN

ALLELUIA - Ad libitum

BCP, p. 654

PROPER 6 A

REFRAIN

We are his peo - ple and the sheep of his pas-ture.

PSALM 100   TONE IIIb

1 *Be jöy* - ful in the LÓRD, all yöu lands;*
     serve the LORD with gladness
     and come before his pres - / ence wíth a song.

                                    REFRAIN

2 *Know this:* the LÓRD him-self ïs God;*
     he himself has made us, and we are his;
     we are his people and the sheep of / his pás-ture.

                                    REFRAIN

3 *En - tër* his gates with thanksgiving;
     go ín-to his coúrts wïth praise;*
     give thanks to him and call / up-on his Name.

                                    REFRAIN

4 *For thë* LORD is good;
     his mercy is év-er-lást-ing;*
     and his faithfulness endures / from age to age.

                                    REFRAIN

ALLELUIA - Ad libitum   *BCP, p. 729*

PROPER 7 A

REFRAIN

An-swer me, O God, in your great mer - cy.

PSALM 69   TONE IVe

7 *Let not* those who hope in you be put to shame
                          through / me, Lord GÓD of hosts;*
   let not those who seek you be disgraced because
                          of me, / O God öf Ís-rä-el.
8 Surely, for your sake have I suf - / fered re-próach,*
   and shame / has cov-ered mÿ face.
                                        REFRAIN

9 *I have* become a stranger to / my own kín-dred,*
   an alien to / my moth-ër's chil-dren.
10 Zeal for your house has eat - / en me úp;*
   the scorn of those who scorn you has / fall-en
                          up-ön me.
                                        REFRAIN

16 *Save me* from the mire; / do not lét me sink;*
   let me be rescued from those who hate me
   and out / of the deep wä-ters.
18 Answer me, O LORD, / for your lóve is kind;*
   in your great com - / pas-sion, turn tö me.
                                        REFRAIN

ALLELUIA - Ad libitum

BCP, p. 679

PROPER 8 A

REFRAIN

Your love, O Lord, for ev - er will I sing.

PSALM 89   TONE V*a*

1 *Your love,* O LORD, for ever will I síng;*
      from age to age my mouth will pro-cláim your
                        fáith-ful-ness.
2 For I am persuaded that your love is established
                        for év-er;*
      you have set your faithfulness firmly iń the héav-ens.

                        REFRAIN

6 *For who* in the skies can be compared to the LÓRD?*
      who is like the LÓRD a-móng the gods?
7 God is much to be feared in the council of the
                        hó-ly ones,*
      great and terrible to all those roúnd a-bóut him.

                        REFRAIN

15 *Hap - py* are the people who know the fés-tal shout!*
      they walk, O LORD, in the líght of your prés-ence.
16 They rejoice daily in your Náme;*
      they are jubilant iń your ríght-eous-ness.

                        REFRAIN

17 *For you* are the glory of their stréngth,*
      and by your favor our míght is ex-ált-ed.
18 Truly, the LORD is our rúl-er;*
      the Holy One of Ís-ra-el iś our King.

                        REFRAIN

ALLELUIA - Ad libitum   *BCP, p. 713*

PROPER 9 A

REFRAIN

I will ex-alt you, O God, my King,

and bless your Name for ev-er and ev-er.

PSALM 145   TONE VI

8 *The LÖRD* is gracious and full of / com-pás-sion,*
    slow to anger and / of grëat kiǹd-ness.
9 The LORD is loving / to eve-ry one*
    and his compassion is o - / ver äll hís works.

REFRAIN

10 *All yöur* works praise / you, Ó LORD,*
    and your faithful / ser-vaǹts bléss you.
11 They make known the glory of / your kiǹg-dom*
    and speak / of yöur pów-er.

REFRAIN

12 *That the* peoples may know of / your pów-er*
    and the glorious splendor / of yöur kiǹg-dom.
13 Your kingdom is an everlast - / ing kiǹg-dom;*
    your dominion endures through - / out äll áḡ-es.

REFRAIN

ALLELUIA - Ad libitum   *BCP*, p. 802

PROPER 10 A

REFRAIN

Let the val - leys shout for joy and sing.

PSALM 65

TONE VIIb

9 *Yöu vïs* - it the earth and water it abundantly;
   you make it vér-y plén-te-ous;*
      the river of God is full of wa-ter.
10 —— Yóu pre-páre the grain,*
   for so you pro-víde for thé earth.

REFRAIN

11 *Yöu dränch* the furrows and smooth out the rid-ges;*
   with heavy rain you soften the grounds and
                     bléss its in-crease.
12 You crown the yéar with your good-ness,*
   and your paths o-ver-flów with plén-ty.

REFRAIN

13 *Mäy the* fields of the wilderness be rich for gráz-ing,*
   and the hills be clóthed with joy.
14 May the meadows cover themselves with flocks,
   and the valleys clóak them-sélves with grain;*
      let them shóut for jóy and sing.

REFRAIN

ALLELUIA - Ad libitum   *BCP, p. 673*

PROPER 11 A

REFRAIN

You, O Lord, are good and for - giv - ing.

PSALM 86   TONE VIIIc

11 *Teach me* your way, O LORD,
    and I will walk in your trúth;*
      knit my heart to you that / I may feár your Name.
12 I will thank you, O LORD my God, with áll my heart,*
    and glorify your / Name for év-er-more.

                           REFRAIN

13 *For great* is your lóve toward me;*
      you have delivered me from the / neth-er-móst Pit.
14 The arrogant rise up against me, O God,
    and a band of violent men séeks my life;*
      they have not set / you be-fóre their eyes.

                           REFRAIN

16 *Turn to* me and have mercy up-ón me;*
      give your strength to your servant;
      and save the child / of your hánd-maid.
17 Show me a sign of your favor,
    so that those who hate me may see it and be a-shámed;*
      because you, O LORD, have helped me
                   and / com-fort-éd me.

                           REFRAIN

ALLELUIA - Ad libitum   *BCP, p. 710*

PROPER 12 A

REFRAIN

When your word goes forth it gives light.

PSALM 119   TONE I*g*

129 *Your de* - —— crées are wón-der-ful;*
    therefore I obey / them with áll my heart.
130 When your word goes fórth it gíves light;*
    it gives understanding / to the sím-ple.

                                        REFRAIN

131 *I ö* - —— pén my móuth and pant;*
    I long for / your com-mánd-ments.
132 Turn to me in mér-cy,*
    as you always do to / those who lóve your Name.

                                        REFRAIN

133 *Stead - ÿ* my fóot-steps ín your word;*
    let no iniquity have do - / min-ion ö-ver me.
134 Rescue me from thóse who op-préss me,*
    and I will keep / your com-mánd-ments.

                                        REFRAIN

135 *Let yöur* countenance shine up-ón your sér-vant*
    and teach / me your stát-utes.
136 My eýes shed stréams of tears,*
    because people / do not kéép your law.

                                        REFRAIN

ALLELUIA - Ad libitum   *BCP, p. 774*

PROPER 13 A

REFRAIN

The Lord rained down man‑na from heav‑en.

PSALM 78   TONE II

14 *He led* them with a cloud by day,*
    and all the night through with / a glów of fire.
15 He split the hard rocks in the wíl‑der‑ness*
    and gave them drink as from / the gréat deep.

REFRAIN

17 *But they* went on sinning a‑gáinst him,*
    rebelling in the desert against / the Móst High.
18 They tested God in their heárts,*
    demanding food for / their cráv‑ing.

REFRAIN

19 *They railed* against God and sáid,*
    "Can God set a table in / the wíl‑der‑ness?"
23 So he commanded the clouds a‑bove*
    and opened the doors / of heáv‑en.

REFRAIN

24 *He rained* down manna upon them to eát*
    and gave them grain / from heáv‑en.
25 So mortals ate the bread of án‑gels;*
    he provided for / them foód e‑nough.

REFRAIN

ALLELUIA - Ad libitum   *BCP, p. 696*

PROPER 14 A

REFRAIN

The Lord shall give strength to his peo-ple.

PSALM 29   TONE IIIb

3 *The voïce* of the LORD is upon the waters;
   the God of gló-ry thún-ders;*
      the LORD is upon the might – / y wá-ters.
4 The voice of the LORD is a pów-er-fúl voice;*
      the voice of the LORD is a voice / of splén-dor.

REFRAIN

5 *The voïce* of the LORD bréaks the cé-där trees;*
      the LORD breaks the cedars / of Lé-ba-non.
7 The voice of the LORD splits the flames of fire;
   the voice of the LORD shákes the wíl-dër-ness;*
      the LORD shakes the wilderness / of Ká-desh.

REFRAIN

8 *The voïce* of the LORD mákes the oák trëes writhe*
      and strips / the fór-ests bare.
9 And in the tém-ple óf thë LORD*
      all are cry – / ing, "Gló-ry!"

REFRAIN

10 *The LÖRD* sits en-thróned a-bóve thë flood;*
      the LORD sits enthroned as King / for év-er-more.
11 The LORD shall give stréngth to his pëo-ple;*
      the LORD shall give his people the bless – / ing
            óf peace.

REFRAIN

ALLELUIA - Ad libitum   *BCP, p. 620*

REFRAIN

Let the peo-ples praise you, O God;

let all the peo-ples praise you.

PSALM 67   TONE IVₑ

1 *May God* be merciful to / us and bléss us,*
    show us the light of his coun - / te-nance aṅd
                cóme tö us.
2 Let your ways be known / up-on eárth,*
    your saving health / a-mong äll ṅä-tions.

                                REFRAIN

4 *Let the* nations be / glad and siṅg for joy,*
    for you judge the peoples with equity
    and guide all the / na-tions üp-oṅ earth.

                                REFRAIN

6 *The earth* has brought / forth her iṅ-crease;*
    may God, our own God, / give us hiṡ bléṡs-ing.
7 May God give / us his bléss-ing,*
    and may all the ends of the earth / stand in
               aẅe öf him.

                                REFRAIN

ALLELUIA - Ad libitum   *BCP, p. 675*

PROPER 16 A

REFRAIN

O Lord, your love en-dures for ev - er;

do not a - ban-don the work of your hands.

PSALM 138   TONE V*a*

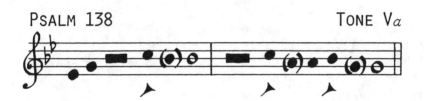

1 *I will* give thanks to you, O LORD, with my whóle heart;*
   before the gods Í will sińg your praise.
2 I will bow down toward your holy temple
  and práise your Name,*
   because of your lóve and fáith-ful-ness.

REFRAIN

3 *For you* have glorified your Náme*
   and your wórd a-bóve all things.
4 When I called, you án-swered me;*
   you increased my stréngth with-iń me.

REFRAIN

7 *Though the* LORD be high, he cares for the lów-ly;*
   he perceives the háugh-ty fróm a-far.
9 The LORD will make good his purpose for mé;*
   O LORD, your lọve endures for ever;
    do not abandon the wórk of yoúr hands.

REFRAIN

ALLELUIA - Ad libitum   *BCP, p. 793*

PROPER 17 A

REFRAIN

Your love, O Lord, is be-fore my eyes.

PSALM 26   TONE VI

1 *Give judg* - ment for me, O LORD,
    for I have lived with / in-tég-ri-ty;*
        I have trusted in the LORD and / have nöt fál-tered.
2 Test me, O LORD, / and trý me;*
    examine / my heärt añd my mind.

                                        REFRAIN

4 *I häve* not sat with / the wórth-less,*
    nor do I consort with / the dë-céit-ful.
5 I have hated the company of e - / vil-dó-ers;*
    I will not sit down / with thë ẅick-ed.

                                        REFRAIN

6 *I will* wash my hands in innocence, / O LÓRD,*
    that I may go in procession / round yöur ál-tar,
7 Singing aloud a song of / thanks-gív-ing*
    and recounting all / your wön-dér-ful deeds.

                                        REFRAIN

8 *LORD, Ï* love the house in which / you dwéll*
    and the place where / your glö-rý a-bides.
12 My foot stands / on lév-el ground;*
    in the full assembly / I ẅill bléss the LORD.

                                        REFRAIN

ALLELUIA - Ad libitum   *BCP, p. 616*

PROPER 18 A

REFRAIN

Make me go in the path of your com-mand-ments,

for that is my de-sire.

PSALM 119   TONE VIIb

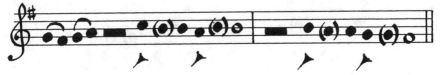

33 *Teach me,* O LORD, the wáy of your stát-utes,*
    and I shall keép it tó the end.
34 Give me understanding, and Í shall keép your law;*
    I shall keép it with áll my heart.

                                                    REFRAIN

35 *Make me* go in the path of yóur com-mánd-ments,*
    for thát is mý de-sire.
36 Incline my heárt to yóur de-crees*
    and nót to ún-just gain.

                                                    REFRAIN

37 *Turn my* eyes from watching whát is wórth-less;*
    give me life in yóur ways.
38 Fulfill your promise tó your sér-vant,*
    which you make to thóse who feár you.

                                                    REFRAIN

39 *Turn a* - way the re-próach which Í dread,*
    because your júdg-ments aŕe good.
40 Behold, I long for yóur com-mánd-ments;*
    In your right-eous-néss pre-sérve my life.

ALLELUIA - Ad libitum   REFRAIN
                                                 BCP, p. 766

PROPER 19 A

REFRAIN

The Lord is full of com-pas-sion and mer-cy,

slow to an-ger and of great kind-ness.

PSALM 103   TONE VIIIg

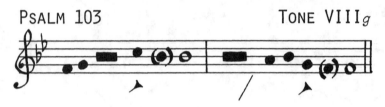

1   *Bless the* LORD, O my soul,*
     and all that is within me, / bless his ho-ly Name.
2   Bless the LORD, O my soul,*
     and forget not / all his ben-e-fits.

REFRAIN

9   *He will* not always ac-cuse us,*
     nor will he keep his an - / ger for ev-er.
10   He has not dealt with us according to our sins,*
     nor rewarded us according / to our wick-ed-ness.

REFRAIN

11   *For as* the heavens are high above the earth,*
     so is his mercy great upon / those who fear him.
12   As far as the east is from the west,*
     so far has he re - / moved our sins from us.

REFRAIN

13   *As a* father cares for his chil-dren,*
     so does the LORD care for / those who fear him.
14   For he himself knows whereof we are made;*
     he remembers / that we are but dust.

ALLELUIA - Ad libitum   REFRAIN
                                            BCP, p. 733

PROPER 20 A

REFRAIN

The Lord is gra-cious and full of com-pas-sion.

PSALM 145   TONE I_g

1 *I will* exalt yóu, O Gód my King,*
      and bless your Name for ev - / er and év-er.
2 Every dáy will I bléss you*
      and praise your Name for ev - / er and év-er.

                                        REFRAIN

3 *Great is* the LORD and gréat-ly tó be praised;*
      there is no end / to his gréat-ness.
4 One generation shall praise your wórks to an-óth-er*
      and shall de - / clare your pów-er.

                                        REFRAIN

5 *I will* ponder the glorious splendor óf your má-jes-ty*
      and / all your már-vel-ous works.
6 They shall speak of the míght of your wón-drous acts,*
      and I will tell / of your gréat-ness.

                                        REFRAIN

7 *They shall* publish the remembrance of yóur great
                  góod-ness;*
      they shall sing / of your ríght-eous deeds.
8 The LORD is gracious and fúll of com-pás-sion,*
      slow to anger and / of great kínd-ness.

                                        REFRAIN

ALI FLUTA - Ad libitum   *BCP, p. 801*

PROPER 21 A

REFRAIN

Re-mem-ber, O Lord, your com-pas-sion and love,

for they are from ev-er-last-ing.

PSALM 25   TONE II

3 *Show me* your wáys, O LORD,*
   and teach / me yóur paths.
4 Lead me in your truth and téach me,*
   for you are the God of my salvation;
   in you have I trusted all / the dáy long.

                                        REFRAIN

6 *Re - mem -* ber not the sins of my youth and my
                      trans-grés-sions;*
   remember me according to your love
   and for the sake of your good - / ness, Ó LORD.
7 Gracious and upright is the LÓRD;*
   therefore he teaches sinners / in hís way.

                                        REFRAIN

8 *He guides* the humble in dó-ing right*
   and teaches his way to / the lów-ly.
9 All the paths of the LORD are love and fáith-ful-ness*
   to those who keep his covenant and his
                      tes - / ti-mó-nies.

                                        REFRAIN

ALLELUIA - Ad libitum   *BCP, p. 614*

PROPER 22 A

REFRAIN

The vine-yard of the Lord of hosts

is the house of Is-ra-el.

PSALM 80   TONE III*b*

8 *You have* brought a vine out of E-gypt;*
   you cast out the nations / and plánt-ed it.
9 You pre-páred the gróund för it;*
   it took root / and fílled the land.

                                        REFRAIN

10 *The moun* - tains were covered bý its shá-dow*
   and the towering cedar trees / by íts boughs.
11 You stretched out its tén-drils tó thë Sea*
   and its branches to / the Rív-er.

                                        REFRAIN

12 *Why have* you brók-en dówn its wall,*
   so that all who pass by pluck / off íts grapes?
13 The wild boar of the fór-est has ráv-aġed it,*
   and the beasts of the field have grazed / up-ón it.

                                        REFRAIN

14 *Turn now*, O God of hosts, look down from heaven;
   be-hóld and ténd this vine;*
   preserve what your right hand / has plánt-ed.
17 And so will we never túrn a-wáy fröm you;*
   give us life, that we may call / up-ón your Name.

ALLELUIA - Ad libitum   REFRAIN
                                        BCP, p. 703

PROPER 23 A

REFRAIN

I will dwell in the house of the Lord for ev-er.

PSALM 23   TONE IV*e*

1 *The LÖRD* —— / is my shép-herd;*
    I / shall not bë ïn want.
2 He makes me lie down / in green pás-tures*
    and leads me / be-side ẅïll ẅä-ters.

                              REFRAIN

3 *He rë* - —— / vives my sóul*
    and guides me along right path - / ways for
                     his Näme's sake.
4 Though I walk through the valley of the shadow of death,
    I shall / fear no é-vil;*
      for you are with me;
      your rod and your / staff, they cöm-fört me.

                              REFRAIN

5 *You spreäd* a table before me in the presence of / those
                  who tróu-ble me;*
    you have anointed my head with oil,
    and my cup / is run-nïng ö-ver.
6 Surely your goodness and mercy shall follow me
                all the days / of my lífe,*
    and I will dwell in the house / of the LÖRD fór
        ëv-er.

                              REFRAIN

ALLELUIA - Ad libitum   *BCP, p. 612*

PROPER 24 A

REFRAIN

As-cribe to the Lord hon - or and power.

PSALM 96   TONE Va

1 *Sing to* the LORD a new song;*
   sing to the LORD, all the whole earth.
2 Sing to the LORD and bless his Name;*
   proclaim the good news of his sal-va-tion from
   day to day.

                                    REFRAIN

3 *De - clare* his glory among the na-tions*
   and his wonders a-mong all peo-ples.
4 For great is the LORD and greatly to be praised;*
   he is more to be feared than all gods.

                                    REFRAIN

5 *As for* all the gods of the nations, they are but i-dols;*
   but it is the LORD who made the heav-ens.
6 Oh, the majesty and magnificence of his pres-ence!*
   Oh, the power and the splendor of his sanc-tu-ar-y!

                                    REFRAIN

8 *As - cribe* to the LORD the honor due his Name;*
   bring offerings and come in-to his courts.
9 Worship the LORD in the beauty of ho-li-ness;*
   let the whole earth trem-ble be-fore him.

                                    REFRAIN

ALLELUIA - Ad libitum   *BCP, p. 725*

PROPER 25 A

REFRAIN

Hap-py are they whose de-light is in the

law of the Lord.

PSALM 1   TONE VI

1 *Hap - p̈y* are they who have not walked in the
                          counsel of / the ẃick-ed,*
     nor lingered in the way of sinners,
     nor sat in the seats / of thë scórn-ful!
2 Their delight is in the law / of thé LORD,*
     and they meditate on / his läw dáy and night.

                                      REFRAIN

3 *They är̈e* like trees planted by streams of water,
   bearing fruit in due season, with leaves that
                     do / not ẃith-er;*
     everything they / do shäll prós-per.
4 It is not so with / the ẃick-ed;*
     they are like chaff which / the ẅind blóws a-way.

                                      REFRAIN

5 *There - för̈e* the wicked shall not stand upright / when
                   júdg-ment comes,*
     nor the sinner in the council / of thë ríght-eous.
6 For the LORD knows the way of / the ríght-eous,*
     but the way of the / wick-ëd iś doomed.

                                      REFRAIN
ALLELUIA - Ad libitum   *BCP, p. 585*

PROPER 26 A

REFRAIN

Send out your light and your truth,

that they may lead me.

PSALM 43   TONE VIIb

1 *Give judg* - ment for me, O God,
    and defend my cause against an un-gód-ly péo-ple;*
        deliver me from the deceitful and the wick-ed.
2 For you are the God of my strength;
    why have you pút me fróm you?*
        and why do I go so heavily while the en-e-mý
                        op-préss-es me?

                                        REFRAIN

3 *Send out* your light and your truth that théy may
                        lead me,*
    and bring me to your holy hill
    and tó your dwéll-ing;
4 That I may go to the altar of God,
    to the God of my jóy and glád-ness;*
        and on the harp will I give thanks to yóu, O Gód
                        my God.

                                        REFRAIN

5 *Why are* you so full of héav-i-ness, Ó my soul?*
    and why are you so dis-qui-et-éd with-ín me?
6 — Pút your trúst in God;*
    for I will yet give thanks to him,
    who is the help of my cóun-te-nance, ánd my God.

ALLELUIA - Ad libitum   REFRAIN
                                        BCP, p. 644

PROPER 27 A

REFRAIN

O Lord, make haste to help me.

PSALM 70   TONE VIIIg

1 *Be pleased*, O God, to de-lív-er me;*
     O LORD, make / haste to hélp me.
2 Let those who seek my life be ashamed
     and altogether dis-máyed;*
       let those who take pleasure in my misfortune
       draw / back and bé dis-graced.

                                    REFRAIN

3 *Let those* who say to me "Aha!" and gloat over me
                           turn báck,*
     be - / cause they áre a-shamed.
4 Let all who seek you rejoice and be glád in you;*
     let those who love your salvation say for ever,
     / "Great is thé LORD!"

                                    REFRAIN

5 *But as* for me, I am poor and néed-y;*
     come to me speed - / i-ly, Ó God.
6 You are my helper and de-lív-er-er;*
     O LORD, / do not tár-ry.

                                    REFRAIN

                                    BCP, p. 682

PROPER 27 A

ALLELUIA VIII

Al-le -lu -ia, al-le-lu -ia, al -le-lu-ia.

VERSE (Matt. 24:42,44)   TONE VIIIg

Be watch-ful and read-y,* for you know not

when the Son of Man is com-ing.

PROPER 28 A

REFRAIN

Teach us to num-ber our days

that we may ap-ply our hearts to wis-dom.

PSALM 90   TONE VIIIg

1 *Lord, you* have been our réf-uge*
  from one generation / to an-óth-er.
2 Before the mountains were brought forth,
  or the land and the eárth were born,*
  from age to / age you áre God.
                                    REFRAIN

3 *You turn* us back to the dust and sáy,*
  "Go / back, O child of earth."
4 For a thousand years in your sight are like
                    yesterday when it is pást*
  and like a / watch in thé night.
                                    REFRAIN

5 *You sweep* us away like a dréam;*
  we fade away sud - / den-ly líke the grass.
6 In the morning it is green and flóur-ish-es;*
  in the evening it is dried / up and wíth-ered.
                                    REFRAIN

7 *For we* consume away in your dis-pléas-ure;*
  we are afraid because of your wrathful / in-dig-
                    ná-tion.
8 Our iniquities you have set be-fóre you,*
  and our secret sin in the light / of your
                    cóun-te-nance.   REFRAIN

BCP, p. 717

ALLELUIA II

Al -le-lu-ia, al-le-lu-ia, al-le-lu-ia.

VERSE (Rev. 2:10)   TONE II

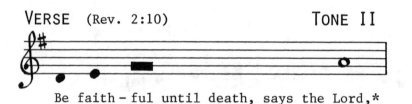

Be faith - ful until death, says the Lord,*

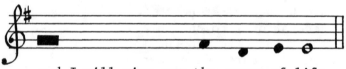

and I will give you the crown of life.

PROPER 29 A

REFRAIN

We are the peo-ple of his pas-ture

and the sheep of his hand.

PSALM 95   TONE VIIIg

1 *Come, let* us sing to the LORD;*
      let us shout for joy to the Rock of / our
                        sal-vá-tion.
2 Let us come before his presence with thanks-giv-ing*
      and raise a loud / shout to him with psalms.

                                    REFRAIN

3 *For the* LORD is a gréat God,*
      and a great / King a-bóve all gods.
4 In his hand are the caverns of the eárth,*
      and the heights of the hills / are his ál-so.

                                    REFRAIN

5 *The sea* is his, for he máde it,*
      and his hands have mold - / ed the dŕy land.
6 Come, let us bow down, and bénd the knee,*
      and kneel before the / LORD our Mák-er.

                                    REFRAIN

(continued)   BCP, p. 724

REFRAIN

We are the peo-ple of his   pas-ture

and the sheep of his hand.

PSALM 95   TONE VIII*g*

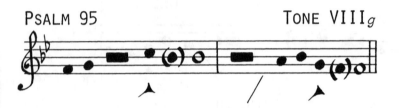

7 *For he* is our God,
   and we are the people of his pasture and the
                  sheep of his hánd.*
  Oh, that today you would / heark-en tó his voice !

                      REFRAIN

BCP, p. 724

Proper 29 A

Alleluia VII

Al-le-lu -ia, al -le -lu -ia, al -le - lu-ia.

Verse (Mark 11:10)   Tone VII*b*

Bless - ed is the kingdom of our father Da-vid

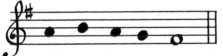

that is com-ing;* blessed is he who comes in

the name of the Lord.

ALLELUIA VERSES

Ad Libitum

ALLELUIA VERSES

For use *ad libitum* when appointed in the Proper.
Any of the verses appointed for particular days
or seasons may also be used, provided that it is
congruent with the Gospel Reading which follows.

1. Show me your ways, O Lord;*
   lead me in your truth and teach me.   *(Psalm 25:3,4)*

2. I will bless the Lord at all times;*
   his praise shall ever be in my mouth.   *(Psalm 34:1)*

3. Your love, O Lord, for ever will I sing;*
   from age to age my mouth will proclaim   *(Psalm 89:1)*
   your faithfulness.

4. Sing to the Lord and bless his Name;*
   proclaim the good news of his salvation
   from day to day.   *(Psalm 96:2)*

5. The commandments of the Lord are sure;*
   they stand fast for ever and ever.   *(Psalm 111:7,8)*

6. Open my eyes, O Lord,*
   that I may see the wonders of your law.   *(Psalm 119:18)*

7. Give me understanding, O Lord,*
   and I shall keep your law with all
   my heart.   *(Psalm 119:34)*

8. Your word is a lantern to my feet*
   and a light upon my path.   *(Psalm 119:105)*

9. The Lord is faithful in all his words*
   and merciful in all his deeds.   *(Psalm 145:14)*

10. How good it is to sing praises to our God;*
    how pleasant it is to honor him with
    praise.   *(Psalm 147:1)*

11. Worship the Lord, O Jerusalem;*
    praise your God, O Zion.   *(Psalm 147:13)*

(continued)

12. Man shall not live by bread alone,*
    but by every word that proceeds from
    the mouth of God.   *(Matt. 4:4)*

13. Your words, O Lord, are spirit and life;*
    you have the words of everlasting life.   *(John 6:63,68)*

14. The word of the Lord stands fast for ever;*
    his word is the Gospel preached to you.   *(1 Peter 1:25)*

ALLELUIA II

Al - le-lu-ia, al-le-lu-ia, al-le-lu-ia.

VERSE (Psalm 25:3,4)   TONE II

Show me your ways, O Lord;* lead me in your truth

and teach me.

ALLELUIA I

Al-le-lu - ia, al-le-lu - ia, al-le - lu-ia.

VERSE (Psalm 34:1)   TONE I*f*

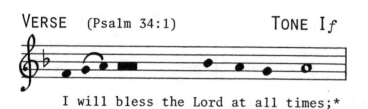

I will bless the Lord at all times;*

his praise shall ev-er be in my mouth.

AD LIBITUM 3 - PSALM 89:1

ALLELUIA V

Al-le-lu-ia, al-le-lu - ia,   al - le - lu-ia.

VERSE (Psalm 89:1)   TONE V*a*

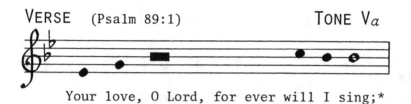

Your love, O Lord, for ever will I sing;*

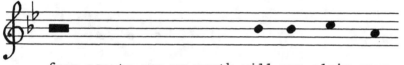

from age to age my mouth will pro-claim your

faith-ful-ness.

AD LIBITUM 4 - PSALM 96:2

ALLELUIA II

Al - le-lu-ia, al-le-lu-ia, al-le-lu-ia.

VERSE   (Psalm 96:2)   TONE II

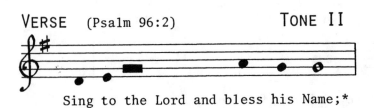

Sing to the Lord and bless his Name;*

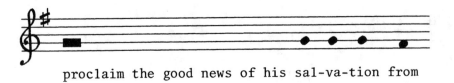

proclaim the good news of his sal-va-tion from

day to day.

Alleluia VII

Al-le-lu - ia, al - le - lu - ia, al - le - lu-ia.

Verse   (Psalm 111:7,8)   Tone VIIb

The   com - mandments of the Lord are sure;*

they stand fast for ev-er and ev-er.

Alleluia VIII

Al-le - lu - ia, al-le-lu - ia, al - le-lu-ia.

Verse (Psalm 119:18)   **Tone VIII**_g_

O - pen my eyes, O Lord,* that I may see the

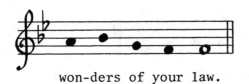

won-ders of your law.

ALLELUIA VI

Al-le-lu-ia, al - le-lu-ia, al-le - lu - ia.

VERSE (Psalm 119:34)   TONE VI

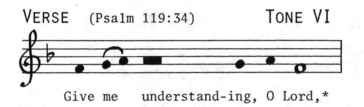

Give me   understand-ing, O Lord,*

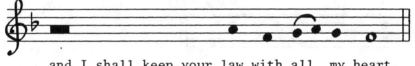

and I shall keep your law with all my heart.

AD LIBITUM 8 - PSALM 119:105

ALLELUIA VI

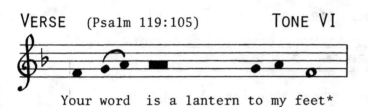

Al-le-lu-ia, al - le-lu-ia, al-le - lu - ia.

VERSE (Psalm 119:105)   TONE VI

Your word is a lantern to my feet*

and a light up-on my path.

ALLELUIA III

Al-le - lu - ia, al-le - lu-ia, al-le - lu-ia.

VERSE (Psalm 145:14)   TONE IIIα

The Lord is faith-ful in all his words*

and merciful in all his deeds.

Ad Libitum 10 - Psalm 147:1

Alleluia I

Al-le-lu - ia, al-le-lu - ia, al-le - lu-ia.

Verse (Psalm 147:1)   Tone I*f*

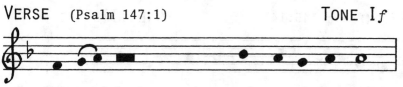

How good it is to sing prais-es to our God;*

how pleasant it is to hon-or him with praise.

ALLELUIA IV

Al-le-lu-ia, al-le - lu - ia, al-le - lu-ia.

VERSE (Psalm 147:13)   TONE IV*e*

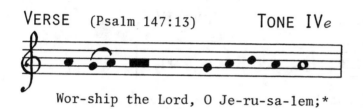

Wor-ship the Lord, O Je-ru-sa-lem;*

praise your God, O   Zi - on.

AD LIBITUM 12 - MATT. 4:4

ALLELUIA IV

Al-le-lu-ia, al-le - lu - ia, al-le-lu - ia.

VERSE (Matt. 4:4)   TONE IV*e*

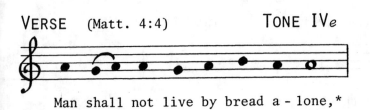

Man shall not live by bread a - lone,*

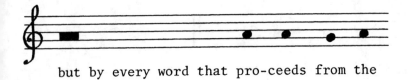

but by every word that pro-ceeds from the

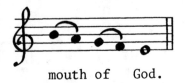

mouth of   God.

AD LIBITUM 13 — JOHN 6:63,68

ALLELUIA VII

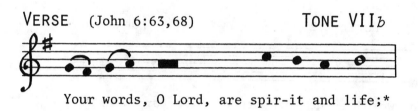

Al-le-lu - ia, al - le - lu - ia, al - le - lu-ia.

VERSE (John 6:63,68)   TONE VIIb

Your words, O Lord, are spir-it and life;*

you have the words of ev-er-last-ing life.

AD LIBITUM 14 - 1 PETER 1:25

ALLELUIA V

Al-le-lu-ia, al-le-lu - ia, al - le - lu-ia.

VERSE (1 Peter 1:25)   TONE Va

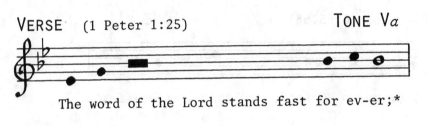

The word of the Lord stands fast for ev-er;*

his word is the Gos-pel preached to you.